ALL IN A LIFETIME

Helen Howington

authorHOUSE®

AuthorHouse™
1663 Liberty Drive
Bloomington, IN 47403
www.authorhouse.com
Phone: 1-800-839-8640

First published by AuthorHouse   11/17/2010

ISBN: 978-1-4520-6764-3 (sc)
ISBN: 978-1-4520-6766-7 (hc)
ISBN: 978-1-4520-6767-4 (e)

Library of Congress Control Number: 2010912452

Printed in the United States of America

This book is printed on acid-free paper.

THIS BOOK IS DEDICATED TO MY PARENTS EVA AND FRANK, WHO BRAVELY OVERCAME THEIR FEARS AND CROSSED THE OCEAN TO START THEIR NEW LIFE IN A FOREIGN COUNTRY. AND TO THE REST OF MY WONDERFUL FAMILY AND FRIENDS, WHO ALWAYS SEEMED TO BE THERE.

ALL IN A LIFETIME

Life deals the cards, and you can play the game of chance in a world full of many opportunities and struggles. Everyone wants to come out on top and be a winner as he or she participates in the events of a lifetime. Come along and enjoy the ride of your life, with heartwarming experiences as we travel past time in this poignant story. You will be sure to find lots of true courage, undying love, hearty laughter, and bitter tears in a life on the lam from the immigration police. The ride may sometimes appear to be bumpy, but it's well known that, with the love and trust in God, hard work, determination, and a great deal of patience, sweet success and lots of happiness is available to all who seek out the best life has to offer. How true are the words heard many times—"Only in America."

Frank and Eva's true and heartwarming life saga begins in 1915, continues over the twentieth century, and tells of their children's lives. The adventure begins in the southeastern corner of Poland, just twenty miles from the Ukrainian border in the very quaint villages of Szkary and Sanok. This is close to the Carpathian Mountains and the Ukraine. Frank was born in 1899, and Eva was born in 1903.

CLIMB ABOARD AND ENJOY THE RIDE AS YOU TURN THE PAGES

In the mornings when Eva lived with Helen in Miami, as they were enjoying their coffee, she would tell her daughter stories about her childhood experiences in Europe. Helen was an attentive listener as Eva shared stories about her past life in the Ukraine, Poland, and, later, America.

Traveling back in time, you can picture Eva as a young lady of twelve with long blonde hair, bright rosy cheeks, and soft hazel eyes. She lived comfortably on a small farm with her family. You almost feel chilled when you think about the long, cold winters with the heavy, icy snowstorms. Many times, they were trapped in their homes as the heavy snow covered the windows and piled heavily high above the rooftops.

Her family lived in a little cottage with a dirt floor on a small farm in Sanoku, and they had to go out into the cold night air to use the outside toilet. One evening as Eva stepped out the door, she spotted an animal with bright, shining, green eyes that looked like a dog. The animal sat very still, watching her every movement, and she quickly ran into the house to tell her mother about the beautiful dog she had just seen. Speeding out the front door, her mom gave a quick look and spotted the wolf as he made a speedy getaway into the nearby woods. Her mom told her how lucky she was not to have been attacked or eaten by the hungry wolf. It was a close call for Eva, and she was reminded to be more careful going outdoors day or night in the winter, as the wolves were very hungry and always busy searching for food. They were ready to pounce on their prey, even small children.

Many times, it was necessary for Eva to go down to a nearby stream and use the rocks to wash some of her clothes, and sometimes the current was so strong that it carried her clothes downstream. It was a hard life, but they were strong-willed and took each day with stride in their desire to enjoy life and survive.

On one occasion, Eva talked about the time when some soldiers came over to her house looking for food during a time of war. The soldiers took all their animals except some of the sheep that were hidden in a small shed farther out back of the home. After a great deal of pleading by Eva's mom, they left without her favorite milk cow, and the family was unharmed.

Eva talked to her grandchildren about her many experiences as she reminisced about her days gone past. She had loved to ride bareback on her beautiful horse, and you could almost picture her flying bareback through the woods at great speeds.

Eva mentioned that, when she was a young girl, she would walk into the woods and pick giant strawberries. The family's vegetables grew big and sweet, as the land was covered with rich, black dirt. Eva would collect the eggs from the hens, taking them along with the strawberries to town with her brother Andrew. At the market, she would trade their wares for much needed items.

One day, Eva and Andrew had a most chilling experience when they went to the city to trade off some of their tasty strawberries. In the town square, some of the villagers were being lined up in full view, waiting to be shot by invading soldiers. Sadly, some of the townspeople were standing in the line of fire and were being killed. Evan and Andrew fearfully watched as the soldiers began to run out of bullets, quickly turning to their bayonets. The siblings were the last in line, and they waited for the sound of the bullets .As they stood in terror, they begged to stay alive, and their prayers were answered. As the soldiers ran out of firepower, they felt a bit of compassion and decided to spare the young brother and sister, letting the pair go free.

In 1918, the plague (influenza) followed the war, killing approximately forty million people. Much of the population left their homes and went in uncovered wagon trains to stay in Russia. Frank's father had been away on a short trip and, upon his return, found his family had also gone to Russia. It was too late to leave with the others, so he stayed home alone to take care of the farm. As conditions improved three years later, the people were encouraged to return home to their villages.

An important part of the family history of interest was that Eva's mom's first husband had hurt his leg. The leg had later become infected and, as a result, it had been amputated. He'd died a short time later, since his leg did not heal properly as a result of an infection. After Eva's mom remarried, she found her new husband acting irresponsibly, and she was then forced to care for the farm and family. Her new husband would go back and forth to America to seek his good fortune. When he made money, he would not consider the needs of the household but spent it foolishly or just gave it away.

Eva worked hard on the farm, always helping her mother by milking the cows, planting vegetables, feeding the animals, and herding the sheep. There were many times when Eva's sisters were spiteful and showed their jealousy because of the special attention their mother had shown to their sister. They found joy in hiding Eva's pretty headscarves when she wanted to go anywhere and many times caused her to stay at home. By the time Eva reached twenty-one she was considered an old maid, as most young ladies of her time were married with families of their own by that age. There was no doubt she could turn a lot of heads with her good looks and a gift to talk, and it seemed like she always had such interesting stories to tell. There was no big hurry for her to leave her mother because she knew she was needed at home. Eva's sisters were not helpful and left most of the work for her to do.

Meanwhile, Frank was in the military in the Polish Army, where he found the going was rough. It was difficult for the soldiers as they were wet and cold, poorly fed, and in need of warm clothes on the battlefield.

It later became necessary for Frank to move on. He joined the Russian Army, where he found the conditions were greatly improved.

While on a short army leave, he attended a wedding next door to Eva's farm, which enabled them to meet for the first time. Frank looked tall and handsome in his army uniform with his light brown, wavy hair and shining, brown eyes. The magic spell was in their eyes, and it was love at first sight for Eva and Frank. Very shortly after Frank came home from the army, the couple was married and became sweethearts and loving partners for a lifetime. Their wedding feast was a happy occasion lasting for three days, with good food, dancing, singing, and lots of celebrating.

After the wedding, Frank's parents invited the couple to come live with them and take over the family farm. Ownership of the little farm was signed over to Frank, and this was a real honor. The farm was a family's livelihood and means of survival, as the precious land was handed down from family to family.

Frank and Eva's first child, Mary, was born in October 1926. The trio lived on the farm with Frank's family for three years, barely getting by. Making ends meet was difficult, and the little farm was unable to sustain the whole family.

In 1928, Frank decided to sell his interest in the farm to his brother, Wasil; unkind words had been said between the brothers because his brother wanted to run the farm his way. Frank sold the farm for four hundred dollars, enabling his family to leave the country. Doubtful times were on the horizon, and the economic situation did not look good in America.

It would be a tough time to leave Poland, but Frank and Eva were in search of their golden opportunity, as they joined the many immigrants on their way to unknown territory into a world filled with uncertainty. In 1929, America was in a great depression. Significant drops in the stock markets had caused many people to lose all their money. The people were badly frightened, and everywhere, there was a run on the banks. There were many men who were out of work and in need of relief as they stood in bread lines to feed their families. The timing was not right for immigrants to come to America. Many immigrants had been led to believe that the streets in America were paved with gold.

With their four hundred dollars in hand, Frank, Eva, and little Mary started on their journey to America but would go to Canada first. The family endured heavy seas that made Eva seasick most of the time; it was a trip she would not easily forget. She would remember the long days and nights on the ship, as the boat kept rocking from side to side with the oncoming waves, in the cold, turbulent waters. You could also hear the sounds of discomfort from the other passengers who were suffering seasickness.

Eva realized that it would be difficult to leave her mother behind in Europe as she traveled to another world, so many miles away that it might as well have been on another planet. As the days quickly passed, Eva slept with her mother's picture under her pillow, and three years later, it was difficult for her to accept word of her mother's death. Oh, if only she could just see her and hold her for one more time. It was sad that her mother had passed away, ending their close mother-daughter relationship.

Many years later, Wasil, who was still in Poland, wrote Frank and said, "You won, and I lost," meaning that Frank had made the right choice to give up the farm and move ahead with his family to a foreign country on their voyage across the sea.

In spite of all the extreme hardships, Frank and Eva made a good team and were very happy together for a lifetime.

CANADIAN COUNTRY: CRYSTAL COLD AND SNOWING

Traveling via a ship named *The Baltic-Americana*, Frank, Eva, and Mary arrived in Saskatchewan, a prairie province in Canada. They found a beautiful land, crystal clean and frozen with ice, very similar to the homeland they'd left behind in Poland. Immediately, they were able to find work on a gentleman's farm, as the owner's wife had left him and he needed lots of help. Eva cooked for three other men, and among one of her many duties, milked five cows each day.

Eva gave birth to another daughter, Justina (Tina), in Saskatchewan in May 1928. One morning, Eva was preparing a bath for baby Tina, and in the distance, she could hear a loud commotion made by one of the cows, who seemed to be in a lot of trouble in the field. She hesitated for a few seconds and then made a mad dash to see what was wrong. As she immediately raced back, she began to hear baby Tina screaming and found her next to the little tub on the floor. It seems Mary had wanted to bathe her little baby sister, and luckily, Tina had not fallen in the water but outside the tub on the floor. Eva was badly shaken, as it was really a close call.

The family stayed in Saskatchewan for about two years, and during that time, Frank found work in a lumber mill in Kapustasing, Ontario, (pronounced Kapustation). As he was getting very lonely and missed his family, he made arrangements to have Eva join him. They made a mistake and went a day earlier than they had planned, and soon Eva arrived with her cousin and her two girls. They thought it was strange that there was no one waiting for them at the train depot. After waiting a long time, a nice young man from the mill spoke to the ladies, and they told him they were waiting for Frank. After he understood the situation, the young man hurried to the lumber mill with his exciting news. Frank listened as the excited gentleman spoke about a very beautiful lady, her two girls, and cousin waiting all day for someone at the train station. Soon he was on his way to fetch his family, as somehow he knew it was Eva and the girls waiting for him.

Since they found it very difficult living in Kapustasing, they moved again to be closer to the lumber mill where Frank worked. Again, Eva was assigned to washing dishes and doing ladies' work to help out. This enabled her to work while taking care of the two girls, Mary and Tina. Frank was chopping down trees for the mill and was also busy clearing highways full of deep snow.

Sometime during this time, someone was kind enough to give Eva an oversized pink dress. The dress was so large that she needed to tie a string to keep it closed. In the boarding house where she stayed and worked, the owner threw an in-house party for all the tenants. For some unknown reason, he would not allow Eva to attend, and she felt very badly with that left-out feeling. She had really wanted to wear her nice pink dress, with the string holding it closed around her tiny waist.

When Eva's brother, Andrew, arrived from Europe, he asked them to meet him in Montreal, where they could work and stay together. They subsequently rented a home, and to their surprise, found that almost all of the people living in that area spoke French, except for Eva and Frank. After renting a home from a French man, she worked for thirteen men. The times were not easy, and the family had many new hardships to face. Eva needed to wash clothes by hand, and she lifted big, heavy pots and cooked breakfast and dinner for such a large group of people. In the quiet of night, the sounds of the men boarders would get louder and louder. After a lot of heavy drinking, they became a troublesome lot, making lots of noise, as well as throwing glasses at each other. Weary at night, Frank and Eva would just close their door and go to bed as they shut the world out. Inasmuch as it proved to be too much work for Eva, they were only able to stay there for about a year. Luckily, Frank was finally able to get a job in a shop that worked with iron. He had been persistent, returning over and over to ask for the job, and the shop owner finally gave in, putting Frank to work.

On one occasion, two of their guests were visiting, and for some unknown reason, they grew louder and louder and came to physical blows. Not knowing what to do as the fight continued, Eva stood up on a chair to attract their attention. Since that didn't work, she got down from the chair and grabbed one of the men by his shirt and demanded that the fighting stop immediately. Otherwise, they would have to leave and be on their way. As the noise quieted down, the pair was allowed to stay for the rest of the evening. Some of their so-called friends were a bit jealous, and they had to be careful. They always were in fear that the next knock on the door could be the immigration police come to send them back to Europe.

In October 1929, a third daughter, Anna, was born in Quebec. She would later marry a family friend named John, whom she had met in Pennsylvania when she was a little girl. Their children would be John Jr., Frank, and Susan.

A year later, Eva became pregnant, and she had a tough time when she suffered a miscarriage, losing her baby boy in the bathroom. The pain must have been so intense that she passed out and woke up three hours later. Eva, always the great lady, was soon back at work, helping Frank with never a complaint about the many hardships they faced daily.

Frank and Eva were deeply in love and happy to share their life's adventure, though, many times, they wondered what would it be like if they had stayed back home in Europe. Being far away from Poland, they missed their family and ethnic lifestyle. Over a period of time, Frank and Eva felt farther and farther away, but they always believed that with hard work, determination, and faith in God, they would achieve their dreams in America.

On to America: First Stop, Pennsylvania

Frank and Eva's adventure continued, as the time had come for them to carry on with their journey to America—the land of opportunity for so many immigrants who had come before them seeking a better life. They called upon Uncle Mike (Striko), who was Frank's brother, to come to Canada and bring Eva and the three girls, Mary, Tina, and Anna to Pennsylvania by train. They were attempting to get into America illegally, as they were unable to enter the country because of quota limitations at that time, and they needed a sponsor. Frank made plans to meet them after they were safely in America. During their train ride, the conductor kept watching and questioning Eva, clearly suspecting something was amiss. He had surmised that Eva looked too young to be Mike's wife. After enough questioning, the conductor asked them to stop over so he could do a further check into their credentials. Mike went into action immediately, taking out his sheriff's badge and asking not to be questioned any further. The conductor respected the badge and dropped the matter. Mike and Eva knew this had been a close call and were glad that it was over. They went on to Mike's home in Pennsylvania, where they settled in and waited for Frank's arrival.

The Statue of Liberty, So Tall and Proud, Her Bright Torch Welcoming the Crowd

Meanwhile, Frank stayed on in Canada to begin selling the family's belongings. In a short period of time, Frank paid someone to bring him on a boat to America. You can only imagine how terrified he must have been to get in a small boat because he had never learned how to swim. His thoughts were of joining his loving family, who were anxiously waiting for him in Pennsylvania, and his strength and courage prevailed.

Uncle Striko and Aunt Strina had a profitable butcher-deli business and wanted to be close to their family. They rented Frank and Eva an apartment, and the newly reunited couple settled in quickly. Many times, Eva complained that they paid too much for their rental, as it was so very damp and she saw mushrooms growing on the walls. Their complaints went on deaf ears, and they tolerated the mushroom walls for a while longer. They continued to meet with friends and relatives, sharing fun times and playing card games. On occasion, some of the men drank a little too much and would start fighting. It wasn't very long before one of the men stabbed another man, causing him to bleed heavily. Of course, Eva took care of the wound, and they were back to normal, continuing to play cards. With so much commotion, they feared the next knock on the door would be the immigration police sending them back to Europe.

Soon Frank and Eva were on the move again; this time, they rented a small house on Pine Street from some nice friends near Alden in Nanticoke, Pennsylvania. For the next five years, Frank went to work down in the mines in Wilkes-Barre and Nanticoke. Times were difficult, with many work-related problems and numerous strikes. It was a frightening time—some of Frank's co-workers were injured in the fighting, and a few were killed. It seemed Frank's lungs were to become a problem, causing him to move on. As luck would have it, one of their jealous neighbors reported them as illegal immigrants, and their dreaded fear was with them, once again. They knew the next knock on the door could be the immigration police sending them back to Europe. It was time to move on and make their way for a new life in New York. Frank and Eva were on the run again, and this time, they decided to seek a productive life and settle down in Brooklyn.

During their stay in Pennsylvania, Nancy (Anastasia) was born in Nanticoke in 1931. She would later marry, have three children, and finally settle in Florida.

Eva and Frank were happy that they were able to visit many of their friends they had made in Pennsylvania. Their social life many nights included playing cards and enjoying a few drinks.

Brooklyn, New York: A Lot of Hustle and Bustle Await, with Lots to See and Do as They Travel on to Another State

Frank and Eva decided it was time to leave Pennsylvania and the coal mines to search for a new way of life, in a less dangerous job that would provide more security for their growing family. They decided to maintain several exclusive apartment buildings, and Frank became the new janitor in town. Unfortunately, their new job was of a short duration, as some of the tenants began to complain that the children were making too much noise. By this time, the family had grown, and there were four children—Mary, Tina, Nancy, and Anna—to care for.

Frank accepted a new job on Eastern Parkway to take care of some ritzy apartment buildings. The furnaces in the apartment buildings and homes were fueled with coal. He would stoke the furnaces, and there were times he would get heated up before going out into the cold night air. The owner treated the family very kindly and always showed her appreciation in many ways. It turned out to be a much better place to work with nicer living quarters.

The twins, Helen and John, were born in January 1936 at Kings County Hospital.
Frank and Eva hadn't expected twins, but they were most welcomed. Unexpectedly, Frank was hospitalized with double pneumonia three times within a short period of time. Working conditions in the mines were not good and had cause Frank's lungs to weaken. Many a cold night, he had to fuel the furnaces in all the large buildings, causing him to become hot and sweaty. The owner of the building was a kind and a wonderful Jewish lady, who could sense some of the hardships Frank and Eva were bravely facing in their struggle to enjoy their new life and to become American citizens. One day, she questioned Frank as to why he didn't get a better-paying job. He told her of his inability to get a weekly job with good pay.

He was here illegally and unable to apply for a social security card, which he needed to get a good-paying job.

At once, the kind lady assumed responsibility for Frank, Eva, and six children. Happily, they made arrangements to go back to Canada with Mary, Ann, and Tina to reenter the country legally and become American citizens. They were relieved to know they no longer had to fear the immigration police the next time there was a knock on the front door. They finally were Americans, with an open door to a better life for the family. On a beautiful, sunny day while living at Eastern Parkway, Mary, Tina, and Anna went off for a long walk to Prospect Park, quite a distance away. With nary a word to their mother, the girls took the twins, Helen and Johnny, in the baby stroller for their long walk. They were having so much fun that they lost track of time, and when they finally arrived home, their grateful parents welcomed them back with open arms and forgave them. They were home safe, and that was all that mattered. It was amazing that the children hadn't thought ahead and realized that their parents would be worried for their safety.

Each week from their window, the family could hear a man calling out for "any old rags" as he sat on his horse and wagon and rode down the street. Today, it would seem very strange to see such a scene in the city on Eastern Parkway in the middle of the day. Many people did appreciate the rag man as an easy way to get rid of old items. Some peddlers would also ride by with their horses and wagons to sharpen knives for the housewives.

Eva could remember way back when there were iceboxes instead of refrigerators to keep the perishables cool and from spoiling. The iceman would come by and carry the ice blocks up many stairs. It's good to know that the times have changed for the better with the use of many new appliances.

When they were of young school age Tina, Nancy, and Anna went to Fox Chase to visit a few nuns and some friends; the girls stayed for a few short weeks on summer vacation at a home pioneered by a Catholic church in Philadelphia. Luckily, during this time, they were able to make their Holy Communion. At the end of summer, Frank and Eva were in for a big surprise when they arrived to bring the girls home for school. They were informed that the girls had already been enrolled in the private school, and it would be best if they stayed for at least the school year.

One time while at Fox Chase, Nancy and her friend were in the pool bobbing up and down in the water. Soon they were in too deep and got scared as they began to go under. They were lucky as they needed immediate help and when they called out, Tina just happened to be walking by. She did not hesitate and jumped right in, though she did not know how to swim, helping the girls out of the pool.

Frank and Eva were convinced that it would be in the girls' best interest to stay a while longer. Of course, the trio was homesick and missed the rest of the family; a few times, the girls were allowed to take a bus ride home to Brooklyn for a few days. They made new friends and seemed to enjoy being at the school. It also enabled them to get an excellent education in a private school. The girls felt better as they knew their parents would come to visit with them, and they would be going home in a short while. Three years later, they would be able to return home to their family in Brooklyn from Fox Chase in Philadelphia.

After they had enrolled in school, life returned to normal for Tina, Anna, and Nancy. Their apartment was on the first floor, which was directly behind a Jewish wedding hall. Many nights, the loud sounds of music could be heard blaring through the bedroom window. It didn't take long before the children were out of bed, climbing out the window to take a peek at the wedding celebration. The wedding guests noticed that the girls were outside and began to pass cake and candy through the back window.

One evening, Tony, who was a longtime friend of Frank's and lived and worked at the hall, decided to place the cake close to the back window. Since Mary was having a birthday, the girls decided to bring home some of the wedding cake—the part with the bridal top. As soon as Tony discovered the missing wedding cake top, he rushed over to search for the missing cake. He was very concerned because the cake was needed for the next day's wedding reception. Tony found the partially eaten cake after questioning the girls, and they admitted their folly. The girls knew they were in big trouble, and their dad agreed to replace the wedding cake. You can be sure Mary and her sisters would remember that birthday for a long time to come.

Another time, when Johnny was about eight, he started a small fire in the basement of their downstairs apartment on Eastern Parkway. There was a great deal of commotion with the fire engines on the way, quickly arriving on the scene. Johnny was in a state of shock and promptly disappeared to run for cover. He hid under the bed for fear of the firemen and the punishment he would have to face. After a lot of coaxing, Dad told Johnny if he would come out from under the bed, he would not be punished. Johnny was scared and white as a sheet when he slowly crept out and appeared in full view of the family. Dad was so happy Johnny was safe and the building had suffered very little damage that he quickly forgave him, and Johnny was lucky that he was able to get out of hot water so easily.

When Helen was about eight years old, she helped a nice older woman look for some of her valuables, which were stashed away in her storage bin. It was very dark in the basement, and Helen lit a candle to get better lighting in the room. Sadly, in a flash, Helen's beautiful, golden, curly locks were set on fire. She ran as fast as she could while crying out loud for her mom's help. Eva quickly doused the fire in Helen's hair under the faucet in the tub. For Helen's help, the nice lady gave her a nickel. And for the price of one nickel, Helen lost her golden curls forever.

Helen remembers that when she was in kindergarten, on rainy days, Frank would take Helen to school on the handlebars of his bicycle, and then it would be Johnny's turn. City blocks were a long walk in Brooklyn, and it seemed like they were the only kids getting a ride to school with their dear father on a bicycle.

After their move from Eastern Parkway, Frank and Eva planned to care for a different large apartment building on Hinsdale Street and Livonia Avenue. Somehow, the owner of their building knew Frank would find a good replacement, since he was leaving. One evening, Frank was out and left Eva home alone with the young twins, Helen and Johnny. Unexpectedly, there was a loud knock on the door. Eva knew the man had to be Frank's replacement, so she welcomed him in. Johnny was up to his usual prankster tricks, turning off all the lights and leaving the house in total darkness.

The stranger thought it was funny and was laughing out loud with his mouth wide open; and in the dark, the stranger's pearly white teeth were visible. Frightened and stunned, Eva and the twins were soon happy to hear Frank at the door. After turning on the lights, Frank wanted to know, "What's going on here?"

Needless to say, they all recovered, and Johnny pretended as if nothing had happened. The stranger with the shiny white teeth became Frank's new replacement, and everything worked out for everybody.

A short time later, the family was able to move on to their new apartment building on Hindsdale Street. The family was in for a big change, they realized, as they listened to the noise of the train overhead, which went by day and night. The loud noise made it almost impossible to get a good night's sleep. It was surprising to note that after two weeks, nobody seemed to notice the noise of the train, as they had adjusted to the rattling of the windows and the shaking of the building. They could finally enjoy their sleep in peace.

THE SECOND WORLD WAR CAME AT A HEAVY COST: SO MANY LIVES WOULD BE DESTROYED AND LOST

There were many times the family knew they were lucky they'd left Poland much earlier. Had they not, they would have possibly been there for the maddening times of the Second World War, as the Germans invaded Poland, with much death and destruction to follow. Frank and Eva were deeply concerned about their families left behind, and many times, Frank checked with the Red Cross for information on his relatives.

On December 7, 1941, the United States of America entered the Second World War, and "Pearl Harbor Day" would go down in history as a tragic time for the entire world. Helen remembers the strange events that happened at home when she was nine. At 9:00 p.m. each evening, loud sirens could be heard as they blared across the city, warning the people to turn off all lights, and smoking was not permitted. The air raid wardens walked the streets, checking each home to ensure that the city was in total darkness. It was lights out, in an attempt to keep the Germans from bombing the citizens in New York City.

Helen remembers when her school gave her a medallion made of bone to be worn on a string around her neck at all times. It was a dangerous time, with the bombings in England and war approaching America. When Helen went to the corner candy store to buy a penny piece of bubblegum, she was surprised when the storekeeper had to remind her that there was a war going on. He asked her how come she didn't know there wasn't any bubblegum available.

During this time, every household was given ration books. Everyone shared and traded them with family and friends so they could buy sugar, meat, and other goods. It was impossible to buy many items, such as appliances, autos, nylons, tires, gas, and other necessities, as they were unavailable. A lot of people were willing to pay much higher prices to the black market crowd, inasmuch as it was so difficult to obtain what they needed. Many of the women worked in factories and navy yards to help in the military war effort, as this was a very difficult time in our history. Everyone pitched in to help, wherever they could, as they were all proud Americans helping out. People bought war bonds to help in the war effort as well.

These were difficult times, as many families lost their loved ones to the war. Frank contributed to the war effort by working at the Brooklyn Navy Yard as a ship builder. He was very talented and could do many different jobs, including carpentry work, electrical work, plumbing, and miscellaneous jobs. With so many good dentists in this country, it wasn't necessary to try and help his friends with their teeth problems as he had in Poland.

Frank and Eva continued working hard and saving as much money as they could. Times were better and things were beginning to look up, and the dream for their own home and security had become a reality. They bought a three-story, brick brownstone on Snedicker Avenue for cash in the amount of three thousand five hundred dollars.
The purchase of their much-needed home was an accomplishment, with a new beginning. It was evident that their faith, determination, and hard work had paid off.

It was 1945, and the bloody war was finally over; the troops were beginning to return home to their waiting families. The time had come for the country to celebrate with block parties and dancing in the streets throughout the neighborhoods. It had been a costly war, but it was over, and the world was finally at peace.

The Second World War found Mary and Tina working in a small factory that bound books on Varick Street, near the Holland Tunnel in New York City. Each day, many trucks full of servicemen came and went through the tunnel. At work, Tina and Mary would drop down little notes from their window into the streets and watch as they sailed into the waiting arms of those good-looking sailors. All the while, they felt safe upstairs hidden from view. Usually, the notes indicated that the young ladies would be waiting downstairs at the side door around 9:00 p.m.

But one time, a sailor named Walter and his friend outsmarted the girls by waiting for them at the front door. Tina and Mary were surprised, but the sailors seemed like nice young men, and the girls agreed to go home on the train with them, giving them a chance to get better acquainted.

From the very beginning, Tina and Walter were attracted to each other. He was on leave from the navy and needed to see Tina once more. Walter's friend had misplaced Tina's address in all of the excitement, but Walter decided to take a big chance and go look for her. Though he thought he might get lost in the big city of Brooklyn, he knew that he had to find Tina and remembered that she lived in a Jewish neighborhood. At first, he went to the wrong New Lots Avenue stop on the BMT. He noticed unfamiliar surroundings as he searched around the train station and then decided to take another train. After he got off on the right New Lots Avenue on the IRT, it was time to start asking people along the way for a Polish family who lived in the area. Hope, determination, and faith helped him to find Tina. They married in September 1945, and were happily married for more than fifty years until Walter's death. Their two lovely girls are Patricia and Linda.

Mary met her husband, Joseph, through friends on Kent Avenue in Brooklyn. They would have six children—Joseph Jr., John, Helen, Gregory, Sophia, and Frankie. The two were meant for each other and would be married for over fifty years until Joe's death.

Frank and Eva were friends for many years with a couple who lived in New Jersey; the couple's son, John would drive his parents down to Brooklyn for a visit. John quickly spotted Anna and immediately took a liking to her. John started making regular trips to Brooklyn, and Anna and John were soon married, in October 1948. They would be happily married for over fifty years until John's death. Their children are John Jr., Frank, and Susan.

At last, the dreaded war was over, and things were getting better for Frank and Eva.

With some help from another neighbor carpenter, Frank was able to join the carpenters' union. He drove many miles out to Long Island to work, and many times it was too hot or too cold to work. Sometimes it was snowing, and he made his long trip to work in vain. Because he had joined the carpenters' union, when he was able to work, he made good pay.

After dinner each evening, the family played cards and listened to the radio for entertainment. The games were Casino and 500 Rummy. It was a family affair and a lot of fun—a good way to pass the time on many cold winter evenings. Helen would play checkers with her dad, and sometimes she would get to win a game or two. Before TV became a part of daily life, the family used to sprawl out on the floor. They would get up close to the radio and let their imaginations work overtime as they listened to *The Shadow, Green Hornet*, and *Let's Pretend*.

In 1948, small televisions began appearing around the country, bringing entertainment into many homes across America. TVs were small, but they made a big difference, and it sure seemed like everyone wanted to own one. Some memorable television personalities were Milton Berle, Ed Sullivan, and Arthur Godfrey with his Lipton Tea commercials; TV stations also featured a wide variety of wild western movies. Each day after work, Frank would stop at a small dry goods store on New Lots Avenue to watch *Captain Video and His Video Rangers*. The program captured his fancy, and he wouldn't miss it, not even for a day,

From the beginning, Frank and Eva's household was one of the fortunate ones to own a small television, and this soon became a problem. Each evening at 6:00 p.m. the doorbell rang. Their neighbor was at the door to watch *Captain Video*. Evidently, he too was hooked and did not want to miss a show. He would appear each night at their front door and stay to watch the TV show and make nasty comments. This went on for some time, and Johnny became so annoyed he decided to take action. Just before 6:00 p.m. the next evening, Johnny shut off all the lights in the home as he patiently waited for the doorbell to ring. He wanted the neighbor to go away, thinking that there wasn't anyone at home. Once again the neighbor was at the front door, but Johnny did not answer the doorbell, prompting the man to buy his own TV set. It was Johnny's good luck that his dad was enjoying his pinochle game at the corner candy store, enabling him to pull off this caper.

Frank was finally able to get a driver's license, and he bought a used, 1946 maroon Dodge auto. He would no longer need his bicycle to help him get around. The family was able to travel in style and visit friends and relatives in the new car. For many years during the Labor Day holidays, they were able to vacation at Striko's fishing lodge in Pennsylvania. It was a long drive from their home in Brooklyn to the beautiful mountains and pristine lakes for fishing and boating at Lake Nuongola, where they had many enjoyable visits with Striko and Strina.

Helen remembers that, when she was a young girl, she would go downstairs to the saloon in the evening when no one was around to enjoy the old player piano. It was easy to play the piano, as she would put some coins into the old machine, and the sounds of beautiful music would fill the room. The room began to feel magical, and she continued to enjoy the music as she surveyed her surroundings. It smelled like a saloon; you could almost taste the beer and liquor upon entering the room. Around a large, walnut bar stood bar stools that could spin around. Featured behind the bar and high stools was a large, mirrored wall. As Helen looked around the bar, she noticed a board on the wall for a game of darts. It was easy to picture the bar full of people as they drank and danced to the old-time music while the player piano played on and on in a magical atmosphere.

The lake was clear and cool and full of summer homes. Many families needed to get away from the city to find some peaceful quiet and natural beauty, as well as to enjoy the good fishing and boating. On a bright and sunny day, Johnny was standing in front of the lake looking down at some of the fish as they swam in the deep water. He seemed to get dizzy and quickly fell in. Cousin Metzie was nearby and heard his call for help; she quickly fished Johnny out. She was unaware that Johnny suffered from epilepsy, a problem that continued to plague him during his lifetime.

At the young age of twenty-eight, Johnny accidentally overdosed on his medicine, and sadly, Helen lost her twin brother.

On many occasions, Striko had some free time and would go hunting for bear in the woods near the lake. One day, he caught a big black bear and had it stuffed standing up.

Though it was dark and the kids were a little afraid, they managed to sneak upstairs to his bedroom and touch the bear to see how it felt. It was nice to pet the furry animal, knowing it couldn't bite or hurt them. The bear was trapped in the upstairs bedroom forever.

RIDING QUAINT TROLLEY CARS: How Romantic they May Be But Sadly, in the Future, They Will Never See

One morning when Helen and Johnny were young children, they were walking close to their home on New Lots Avenue. It was obvious that the quaint trolley tracks were being dug up and were going to be replaced by new, modern buses. Times were changing, and so was the city; they would miss the trolleys. Johnny was having the time of his life throwing rocks across the street, and it wasn't very long before one of the big rocks hit Helen in the head. The blood streaming down her face from the hole in her forehead was a sad sight to see. Imagine the trail of the kids on the block running down the street following her in all the excitement. After the twins made it home in record time, Eva went into immediate action. She quickly filled the hole in Helen's forehead with some milk and bread, and the crying and the bleeding stopped. With Eva's quick thinking and the use of her old time remedies, Helen was okay. Johnny said he was sorry, and all was forgiven, after he realized that he should have listened to her pleas for him to stop.

It's truly amazing how we take our eyesight for granted day by day. Helen was very nearsighted, as well as being very short, causing her to have difficulty seeing the blackboard at school. After Helen read the eye chart, her teacher sent her to the eye doctor for a thorough examination.

Putting on her new glasses, Helen was in awe as she looked around. After carefully stepping off the curb to cross the street, she saw the leaves on the trees for the first time. Knowing that she no longer would have to sit on her feet in the back of the classroom to see the blackboard more clearly was a wonderful feeling.

At the age of twelve, Helen got busy baby-sitting for the children close to home. This gave her spending money and the chance to buy some stylish clothes she wanted to have. This was the start of many important lessons, mainly on the management of money. At an early age, Helen learned that she would carefully save her money for the things she wanted to buy, and learning to become independent was a good feeling.

Sometime in 1950, one night while they were young and living in Brooklyn, Helen and Johnny found that they were locked out of their home. Frank and Eva had been in a hurry to meet with some of their old friends from Europe and they hadn't expected to be gone for long. They'd had good intentions and had meant to get back very shortly. Since Helen had a previously arranged baby-sitting assignment, she had to go. She did not want to leave Johnny alone locked out of the house with their dog Spotty while he waited for their parents to come home. Helen decided to leave the children she was baby-sitting in the care of Adele's downstairs neighbor and go home to check on her brother. Arriving at home, she found Johnny and Spotty in big trouble. She began to think back to an incident earlier in the day when a strange dog had chased her and Spotty as they were crossing Linden Boulevard. The traffic light had suddenly changed to red, and they'd raced across the street, leaving the wild dog behind in the traffic. He must have sniffed out Spotty's scent and returned to their home for the attack.

It was frightening to see her brother, Johnny, standing on a bench upstairs on the porch holding Spotty up in the air high above his head. He was trying his best to protect their dog from being attacked by a wild German shepherd. Helen did not hesitate for a minute; she picked up a small pillow, jumped up on the bench, and went after the dog. Both dogs were growling, and the wild dog was ferocious, biting Helen on her arm. The dogs had caused quite a commotion, which brought out the neighbors. They quickly contained the animal, taking him to the pound where he was checked for rabies. Sadly, no one claimed the dog. Helen was in need of medical attention; she caught a bus on the corner and headed for Beth-El Hospital for treatment. The doctor cauterized the large bite on her upper arm, leaving a large scar that is still visible today. It would always serve as a reminder of how she and Johnny had saved Spotty. With fear in their hearts and quick thinking, Johnny, Helen, and Spotty had come out on top.

After all the excitement was over, Frank and Eva came home. They listened to the night's events in surprise and were so thankful that everything had turned out okay and the kids were safe. After Helen's return from the hospital, she headed down two long city blocks to Adele's home to check on the children she was baby-sitting. When Helen arrived, the children were still asleep. Soon Adele arrived home, and Helen told her of the events that had occurred while she was away. She was truly amazed and was very understanding about the events that had taken place while she had been gone, only a couple of hours.

In 1950 on Valentine's Day, Helen was again baby-sitting and was getting ready to go home. Adele was tired and was in a hurry to get home, and she let the cab go. It was about midnight on a school night, and Helen was half asleep. They walked together to the corner of Linden Boulevard, and Adele asked her to cross the boulevard and go home the rest of the way alone. It was late, and Helen refused to go any farther alone. As they crossed the road, a car came out of nowhere and ran through a red light and knocked them down on the pavement full of cold, slushy snow and ice.

Soon Helen regained consciousness. She felt a funny ringing in her ears and found herself in the middle of Linden Boulevard alongside Adele in the damp, cold, wet snow as cars whizzed by. Some kind city workers had been cleaning the highways of snow and were on their way home to change their wet clothes. They witnessed what happened and immediately were in hot pursuit of the car. They caught the man and insisted that he return to the scene of the hit-and-run accident. The young man indicated that he did not realize that he'd struck the two women, although his lights were out and he had a broken windshield. It was late at night, and many of the neighbors got out of their beds when they heard all of the commotion, quickly bringing some warm blankets to comfort the two women who were lying in the wet street. The ambulance quickly drove the women off to Beth-El-Hospital, and after some X-rays, they told Helen she had suffered a broken pelvic bone. Sadly, Adele was pregnant, and she lost her baby. Because Helen did not have any health insurance, she was quickly transferred to Kings County Hospital for further treatment.

Trapped in a hospital bed, flat on her back, Helen was unable to sit up or feed herself. She found herself parked in a hallway in the overcrowded hospital for ten days. When she woke up the first morning, she heard beautiful singing in the hall. There was a young lady about fifteen years old singing loudly, "There's no tomorrow." This lovely lady had fallen the night before while roller-skating at the rink, injuring her leg. Mickey was kind to Helen.

Each day, she would come by to feed Helen and spend time by her bed. Mickey's kindness brought the girls closer together, creating a longtime friendship. On Saturdays after their injuries were healed, Helen and Mickey would meet halfway at the subway station and visit many fascinating places for excitement in New York City. On many enjoyable nights, Helen was able to stay overnight at Mickey's home.

There was a tradition in the family that every Friday night was movie night. It was a lot of fun adding dishes for their future hope chest. One night, Helen was up to no good and tied a string across the aisle in the darkened theater. A young man innocently walked down the aisle looking for a seat with popcorn in hand. Not seeing the string in the dark, he tripped, sending his popcorn flying everywhere. Not only were his feelings hurt, he was very angry and punched the innocent fellow sitting at the end seat where the string was tied. Helen wanted to disappear as fists started flying. She was sorry and a bit afraid and quickly headed for the back of the movie theater. It didn't take long before a policeman appeared on the scene to break up the fight. Helen learned a valuable lesson, as she realized that someone could have been seriously hurt. She would make sure it would never happen again.

THE LAZY CRAZY DAYS ARE HERE AGAIN: ENJOYING BROOKLYN IN THE SUMMERTIME

Days of long ago, when Frank and Eva's children were young, they found that living in the city could be a lot of fun. School was out for the summer, and the days were long and hot. They needed to find ways to keep busy. Even today, you can almost picture Nancy's friend Rosie helping the kids to play dress-up when they came to her home. Rosie bought crepe paper, so they were able to make cute costumes for the short plays that she had written. Being able to act in one of Rosie's plays was like living in a fantasy world. She enjoyed helping the girls and started early in her life's career, practicing in her dramatic efforts. Helen was always the first in line to play the movie star role, as she always liked to act, sing, and dance, and still does. You can hear Uncle Eddie: "Someday Helen will become a great actress, especially as she knows how to put on her crying act."

The kids on the block enjoyed some summer learning fun as they played school with a young neighbor named Esther. Esther would gather all the willing children off the street onto her porch upstairs and pass out pencils and paper. This enabled her to practice her teaching skills to all the children who were willing to learn. It was nice of Esther to have the patience to spend her time with the young kids on the block. Not only did it keep them busy and out of trouble, her little students were learning. Many thanks go out to a special lady, lovely Miss Esther.

Nancy helped Helen get a job at Beth-El Hospital. She was able to work part time, while continuing at Thomas Jefferson High School. So, at the young age of fifteen, Helen was riding the bus for a nickel and working weekends in many of the hospital's food departments, including the diet kitchen learning how to prepare meals for special diets and the dining room. During this time, Helen would also work with Nancy in the nursery, watching as her sister fixed baby formulas. She also worked in food preparation for the new mothers in the maternity ward. Looking around the nursery, Helen saw a tiny baby in an incubator who weighed slightly over one pound. It was amazing to look around and see such wonderful miracles.

A rare and powerful hurricane in the winter of 1950 surprised people, causing a lot of damage and inconvenience. Before long the electricity went out in the hospital, and it was frightening, as most of the employees were in a hurry to reach home safely. There was no available transportation, not even the buses, and Helen was left alone in the dark night at the hospital. Luckily, Helen was able to reach her father by phone, and she waited for her dad in a nearby darkened candy store.

Several other hospital employees also waited for rides, and the group sat by candlelight inside the candy store. Helen was a bit afraid and kept running outside to search for her dad in the pouring rain. Soon she heard a voice in the far distance calling, "Helen, Helen, where are you?"

She could finally feel safe—her dad had found her, and he took her home. Hearing the howling wind and the driving rain pelt the windows when they stepped into the car was frightening. Very cautiously, they drove home in the raging storm through the darkened streets. All around, they could see downed trees, and broken glass as it splattered all over the road. As they looked around, they saw devastation everywhere.

When they approached home, they could see that the streets were blocked with many large, fallen trees, making it impossible to park in front of their home. It was November, and the time of the year when the temperatures were freezing. It was also cold in the house, and the family had a rough time, forcing them to sleep in their clothes. With the use of a little gas stove, they were able to cook some food, and the oven also provided a little heat, enabling the family to keep warm as they gathered in the kitchen.

Of all the times Striko should decide to leave Pennsylvania for a few days to visit his brother Frank, he'd chosen that one. Within the hour of his stay, he advised the family that he was ready to go elsewhere, as he could not stay and suffer needlessly. He needed a warm bed and conveniences with some electric power.

After ten days had passed, with no sign of any power for all the families on Snedicker Avenue, it was time to take action. Frank reached the power company, and he was told they were very busy, and it might be several weeks before anyone could get there to cut down the trees. It was necessary for the neighbors to first clear the fallen trees in front of their homes before they could make it through. Frank quickly organized a crew of his neighbors to cut down the trees and push them to the side of the street. They all helped, and the electric power was soon turned on. The neighbors planned a block party to celebrate this joyous occasion, feasting and laughing far into the night.

That's My Dog, Spot, Who Seems
to Get around A Lot

After dinner each evening, Frank and Eva would park their car in a rented garage, which was only a few city blocks away, taking Spotty along for an evening walk. On one particular evening, Frank was in a big hurry to get Eva home so he could race over to the candy store to play cards with the boys for a quarter a game. As they separated, Spotty stood still in the middle of the boulevard. He looked at Frank, and then he looked at Eva, not knowing which way to go. As he waited, Spotty was run over by a speeding car, and since he was knocked out and very still, he was left in the street for dead. Frank was busy comforting Eva while pulling her out of the line of traffic, forcing her to go home without Spotty. She was extremely overwrought over the dog and in tears. Very quickly the Department of Sanitation was on the scene, putting Spotty in the truck headed for the dump. A day didn't go by that Eva mentioned hearing Spotty barking far off in the distance. Deep down she knew he was alive somewhere, and he would come back.

Many times, Eva said she saw Spotty passing by the house with a strange woman, and it seemed that he looked up and saw her. After nine months had passed, Johnny came by with some startling news. He had been playing near a local dumpsite and needed Helen to join him in a good look to make sure that he had really found Spotty, without alarming his mother. It was a miracle that Spotty was well and alive, playing with a young boy who Johnny had befriended. The young friend explained that he had found the dog at the dumpsite with a broken leg about nine months earlier.

The family was so happy to find their dog Spotty alive, and they wanted him back. There was a small problem with the boy's mother, as she refused to return the dog to the family. The woman also loved the dog and didn't want to part with him. They called in their family friend, Tony, asking him to help get Spotty back. They asked the boy's dad to meet with Tony, so they could make some arrangements to buy back their long lost dog.

Eagerly, the man accepted thirty-five dollars for Spotty. Eva was so happy to get her little dog friend, Spotty, back home again. Her dreams had come true because she had always felt that he was alive and knew that she had heard him barking many nights. She never gave up hope, knowing that, one day, he would return home. Spotty again felt at home; he started to sniff around the house, picking up his scent in every room. He remembered the family and knew he was home once again. This was a happy time for Spotty and his family. He moved with Eva and Frank to Florida and lived a long time, going to doggie heaven at age fifteen.

The family really liked their friend, Tony. At times, when Tony was lonely, he would call a taxi and bring his dog, Whitey, to visit for a few days. (Whitey was Spotty's mother.) Several years previously, Tony had lent his son a large sum of money to help him solve his immediate money problems. When Tony retired and was no longer working, money was scarce, and he needed some financial assistance. Frank was kind and lent him some money to enable him to continue in the search for his son.

After several weeks with no word from Tony, they became worried. Meanwhile, the New York City police found Frank's name and address in Tony's wallet. They had been looking for his immediate family after they fished him out of the river. There was no trace of any of his family, and the police believed that he might have been murdered. They told Frank it might be best not to continue the search any further. Tony was gone, and they knew he would never be coming to stay with them in Florida.

In 1952, at the age of fifteen, while still in high school, Helen continued working two nights a week and on Saturdays and Sundays at the hospital. It wasn't very long before she had more responsibilities and was running the coffee shop two evenings a week. The time had come to obtain her much-needed experience as a secretary in the business world, which is what she wanted to accomplish. She went on to become very successful as she continued to work.

Helen volunteered her free time after school to work in the office at her school so that she could gain work experience. She hoped she would be placed in an office job. Not long after she started volunteering, a nice lady came to the school office in search of part-time office help. The woman interviewed another girl named Eunice and was very disappointed to learn that Eunice did not have the necessary shorthand skills. Therefore she was unable to hire her. She looked around the office and noticed Helen busy filing papers at her desk. After some discussion, she hired Helen on the spot as a steno-secretary to work two days after school and Saturdays.

The two women left the school together and drove to the store in her car. Helen was overjoyed with her new job in the TV store. She took the bus and train to work after school, so transportation was not a problem. Her starting salary was seventy-five cents per hour. In a few months, her pay was raised to one dollar per hour. The owners were pleased to have her work there. The job was good for Helen, as she was getting experience that would help her in the world of business that was to become her future.

Three months later, Frank decided to move to Florida. Helen hated to leave her new job, but the clean Florida sunshine and beaches would soon be calling.

In 1952, a big change took place in the family's life after Frank took a trip to Miami to look around. He felt it was time to enjoy the warm Florida sunshine. He visited Striko's daughter, Helen, who had written many letters to Uncle Frank, coaxing him to get down and take a look around to see what he was missing. Frank made preparations to move the family to Florida after he returned from his short visit. He and Eva quickly sold their home in Brooklyn to a young veteran for ten thousand dollars, and the family was soon en route to Florida. After they packed the car, they were ready to go and start their new adventure. The older girls were all married, so Frank, Eva, Helen, Johnny, and Spotty were on their way.

You could almost picture the large crowd of friends and neighbors that gathered around the car to say good-bye as they got into the car to leave on a steamy, hot day in June 1952. There was a tearful sendoff and lots of hugs. Their friends and neighbors were sad to see them move away, as they enjoyed having them around. Everyone liked the family, and it had been nice to know that Frank was always available to handle their problems and repairs.

Soon, Frank, Eva, and crew were making their getaway from the busy city life in Brooklyn to their new adventure in the warmth and sun in Florida.

They were lucky they'd sold the home when they had, as timing had been in their favor. It wasn't much later that the area would change for the worse, and soon their nice, three-story brick brownstone would be torn down to make room for a low-cost housing development.

Welcome to Florida, the Sunshine State
Let's Take a Ride to See Before It's Too Late

After what seemed like driving forever, Frank, Eva, Helen, Johnny, and Spotty arrived in Hialeah, in Miami-Dade County, where they stayed with Cousin Helen for a few weeks. They bought a cozy home in Hialeah, painted in a light pink color. They enjoyed looking around and buying new furniture; this would be their new home, where they could retire and enjoy the warmth and sunny beaches. Since all of the homes were painted in light shades of pink, green, and blue, it was like living in a small fairyland. The area was fresh and inviting, surrounded with lots of green grass and a variety of magnificent palm trees. They would be able to buy tropical fruits, including bananas, at a much lower price, since the fruits were more readily available.

Hialeah was well known and famous for horse racing at the beautiful racetrack. The grounds were a sight to see, with flamingos, tropical plants, coconut palm trees, and water fountains with Grecian statues. It was also fun to drive to the track and enjoy its natural, park-like beauty.

When Frank decided to go back to work, he was able to get into construction and build homes. It wasn't long, though, until he retired to enjoy the good life with Eva, which both so richly deserved. They had both worked hard for so many years, and it was finally their turn to enjoy some Florida fun in the sun.

Johnny introduced Frank to the senior citizens' shuffleboard club, where Frank played cards several nights a week and sometimes during the day. Frank enjoyed the games, and many times, he won and took home his prizes. On occasion, Eva would join him for some of the festivities, and life was good for the couple in America.

They could recall traveling a long way from the frigid, cold country on their farm in Poland; living at the lumber mills in Canada; and relocating to the Pennsylvania coalmines. Eva told Helen about the talks she had with her mother in Poland many years ago: Her mother had mentioned that she'd heard about a beautiful, warm country far way in America. It was truly amazing that the family would wind up a world apart from Eva and Frank's homeland in this beautiful tropical land of Florida in their later years. Had her mother known their fate ahead of time?

Making new friends who they liked to visit on Sunday afternoons was fun. Eva spent quality time in her backyard tending fruit trees, including mango, orange, papaya, lemon, grapefruit, and banana. Many varieties of tropical flowers kept her busy in her sun-filled garden all year round. Frank and Eva had found their tropical paradise.

For the very first time, Helen was able to ride on the school bus each day to her new school in Miami, where she would complete her senior year. The school appeared to be in a very different world; it wasn't at all like Thomas Jefferson High School in Brooklyn. Helen met a lot of new friends and enjoyed attending school each day. As she changed classes, it was nice to walk through the Spanish-style, covered courtyards, breathing in the clean, fresh, warm air.

In order for Helen to graduate from high school in Florida, she had to take classes in American history, sewing, and cooking. Many of the students in the American history class were younger eleventh graders and were on the football team. They liked to call her "the nose" and said she was a good sport to handle all the teasing they put her through. It was her favorite class.

There were many days that the teacher would have Helen get up and teach the class. This was a form of punishment because she always had so much to say. One time, he taped her mouth shut with a bandage, in hopes that might keep her quiet. On several occasions, he took her to the principal's office but asked her to wait outside on the bench. He always liked to tease her but did not want her to get into trouble at the school. Naturally, his favorites were the guys on the football team, and he would kid around with them, as well. Many times Jimmy, one of his favorite football players, would fall asleep in class. One afternoon, the coach marched all of the students very quietly outside and let them peek through the classroom windows. When the bell rang, Jimmy woke up, looked around, and heard everyone laughing outside. He knew the jig was up. It looked like he had been found out, and he was red-faced and embarrassed. Another time, Jimmy was asleep in his seat, and the coach lit a match on the side of his shoe. As the class marched outside, once again peeking through the windows, they saw that Jimmy's shoe was on fire. Jimmy was so embarrassed that he immediately doused the fire and sheepishly ran to his next class.

Almost like winding up an alarm clock, you could count on Tina, Walter, and their daughters, Pat and Linda, to make the long drive from their home in Long Island to take their month-long vacation to Florida in February. Their winter visits were especially nice, and everyone had a great time. Walter was always fooling around with his practical jokes. Sometimes he would dig into his pockets, take out some coins, and ask Helen to guess the year and date on the coin. When she gave the right answers, he would give her the coin. The game was fun and a good way to collect some of his money. The whole family would tan in the sun and frolic in the surf at nearby Miami Beach. The warm water felt refreshing as they jumped over the waves. Frank and Eva always looked forward to the month of February, when they could, once again, welcome their children and grandchildren for a visit.

Anna, John, and family, as well as and Nancy, Eddie, and family, came often to visit their parents in Florida from New York and New Jersey. Their daughters up north were lonely for their mom and dad and made the long trip as often as they could.

Though Helen was busy finishing her senior year in high school, she thought it was time to make a little spending money. A few nights a week and on Saturdays, she would walk to a local movie theater in Miami Springs, where she sold candy and worked as a cashier. Though her hourly pay only started at forty cents, she was happy to feel a little independent, earning some spending money. She didn't want to think about her past job in New York, where she'd been earning one dollar per hour. Leaving that job had been such a disappointment for her, but it was a thing of the past.

Graduation day came rather quickly in the summer of 1953. Helen was enjoying her time at school at Miami Jackson High School, and she knew she had to move on. She left her low-paying job to search for more money in a secretarial job she could enjoy. Helen and her friend, Shirley, checked with several job agencies but were unsuccessful in their search for employment, as jobs were hard to find. Tina came down to stay for a while and suggested they knock on doors together as they searched for some work. Immediately, they set out looking for work, walking the streets and knocking on doors in Hialeah's factory district.

Tina found a job in a factory for a short time, and Helen found a job at a foam rubber factory. Things were looking up, as Helen was earning thirty-eight dollars per week and gaining secretarial experience. The owner of the firm kept Helen past five o'clock many times, as he would decide it was time to start writing letters late in the day. Buses were hourly, and many nights, Helen walked home, a long distance of several miles. Her kind dad would stop by and offer her a ride home when she was able to get away from her mean boss.

Helen fondly recalls Frank's sixtieth birthday. She made a birthday cake and lit sixty candles. He was able to blow out all the candles, while Helen and Eva sang "Happy Birthday." It was an emotional time, and the family cried tears of happiness, as Frank told Helen that it was his first birthday cake. They would continue to share other happy birthdays, until Frank passed away at age sixty-nine of lung cancer.

Happily, the dreaded Korean War was ending, bringing many of the servicemen to Miami. Helen had been hoping to join the Waves in the navy when she turned eighteen.
On Sundays, she would busily check out airplanes on display as she visited many surrounding military bases and airfields. One Sunday, she boarded a submarine that was safely docked in the Miami Harbor and walked through it. It turned out to be a painful experience as, on the day after her visit, her leg muscles ached. Maybe submarines would be best suited for sailors.

Helen and her friend, Shirley, from high school enjoyed skating at the roller rink. Sometimes they borrowed Shirley's mom's car and went without having to wait an hour for the city bus. They enjoyed skating at the rink and were able to go several nights a week to enjoy their favorite pastime— dancing to the music on skates.

One evening while skating, Pete noticed Helen in her cute, short, yellow skating outfit and asked her to skate. Of course, Helen quickly accepted the offer from the handsome young marine who was staring at her with those baby blue eyes. He told her that he was from Indiana and stationed at the Opa Locka Marine Base in the Miami area. His friends also enjoyed going to the skating rink, with its feel-at-home atmosphere.

Pete did not have transportation, so he would thumb a ride to Helen's home in Hialeah. Many times, he would arrive soaking wet as the Florida skies had opened up in a sudden downpour of cats and dogs. Helen would wring out his shirt and put it out to dry, as clothes dryers were on the drawing board somewhere in the future.

Three months later, in December 1953, Helen and Pete were married in the Marine Base Chapel at Opa Locka. As she was only seventeen, she needed permission from her parents to marry. It was a whirlwind romance; they had fallen in love and wanted to share their life together. All her plans to enlist in the navy went up in smoke and were so easily forgotten. A small reception followed at Helen's home, and they spent one wonderful night at the Sorrento Hotel in Miami Beach for a short honeymoon. At that time, Pete's service pay was very little, but they carefully managed to make ends meet.

They stayed for three months at Helen's parent's home while Pete finished his tour of duty in the military. After they married, they bought an old car for one hundred dollars, which was a wedding present from Frank and Eva.

Early in the spring, Pete was anxious to get back home to Indiana, and they made plans to get started. It was difficult for Helen to leave her home and parents, but with tears flowing, they said their farewells. Soon, the couple was on the way to Indiana. Though they were broke, they were young and very much in love and knew somehow there would be a good life ahead.

INDIANA: A NEW START AS THEY ROLL ALONG, LISTEN TO THEM SING THEIR HAPPY SONG

Pete and Helen arrived in Lafayette in their beat-up, old car in the spring to find sunny and cold weather. Helen would often find the cold, damp days and nights difficult to get used to after enjoying the balmy weather in Miami. When you are in love, everything seems beautiful, and she ignored the Indiana weather. Since Pete was out of the military, he was able to return to his old job at Alcoa.

Helen found a job immediately at West Lafayette High School as secretary to the principal. She enjoyed working alongside the young teenagers. Many of the students were very bright, and their parents were professors teaching at Purdue University.

In the past, it would have been unusual for the high school to hire an eighteen-year-old young lady. Helen was able to work with the teachers and students, sharing in-office techniques with the young ladies and making a connection from the beginning. Helen was a part of the team, and she was invited to pep rallies, proms, and football games. She stayed for a year but had to leave for a higher paying job. It was nice to know that the school would have a new hiring program and would allow a younger secretary, who would fit in more easily with the students, to work in the office.

Helen worked hard, and she was getting ready to move on to better things. She was able to get a position working for National Homes Acceptance Corporation for an attorney who was a retired army major. There were many stressful times, and working for the major seemed impossible. At that time, she also worked with several other attorneys in the legal department. Her experience became useful as she would become a real estate broker later on in her life, as it enabled her to understand mortgage servicing, loan applications, and the handling of mortgage foreclosures.

To save money, Helen and Pete lived in Lafayette on a farm eight miles into a rural area near the Wabash River. The rent was thirty dollars a month, and that was all they could afford at that time. Helen never dreamed that it would be necessary to go outside and pump water from the well for drinking purposes and carry water to the house for a bath in fifteen below zero weather. Helen had been born in Brooklyn and was a city girl, used to all the city's conveniences, but she was able to accept life's hardships with no complaints. After all, she and Pete were young and so in love.

A Joy So Great That Tears Begin to Flow; This Is the Most Precious Gift I Know

On a very cold and snowy morning—December 7, 1957—Pete and Helen's first child, Margaret Ann, made her appearance, bringing a great deal of happiness into their lives. For those who have the pleasure of knowing her, Margaret Ann still brings happiness. She can reach out and touch people in many wonderful ways.

About a year later, the young family moved to Lima, Ohio, for a period of three months, as Pete had been working as a furnace and air-conditioning salesman. When they arrived, Helen was very surprised to see a horse-driven wagon and hear the sound of hoofbeats going clop, clop early one cold winter morning on the cobblestone streets; it was amazing to watch the horse, as he seemed to know exactly which houses to stop at to deliver the milk. Being reminded of days gone past was a nice feeling.

Pete had been working as a furnace and air-conditioning salesman, but they were unable to stay. Things just didn't work out because of slow sales. In the meantime, Helen worked at Ex-Cello Corp.

They returned to Indiana, as their dear friends, Margaret and Frank, invited them back to re-rent their little home on the farm for fifty dollars per month. In order to get home each day, they traveled across the old covered bridge above the Wabash River (on the Granville Bridge). While they were away, the little farm home had been modernized and had a new bathroom and running water, making it more comfortable and livable.

Usually in the spring, the Wabash would overflow into the river bottoms, making the land fertile and, possibly, ruining the cornfields that were ripe for harvesting. At these times, Helen and Pete would go in the fields to help Frank and Margaret pick the corn before the river was over the banks. Helen was a real city girl and never dreamed she would be living on a farm. It was nice to breathe fresh country air and help their friends in their attempts to get the corn out of the fields before the river did its damage. Help was scarce, as many of the farmers were also working to save their crops from the waters that rushed over the Wabash's banks. Their friends were kind and caring, helping Helen and Pete as much as they could. After

Frank and Margaret slaughtered their Black Angus cows, Helen and Pete bought a quarter of the T-bones at fifteen cents per pound. This would be remembered for a long time to come.

It snowed on many a cold winter night, and you could hear the blustery wind blowing. Pete had a large coon dog he kept outside for hunting. In the quiet of the night, you could hear the dog's loud moaning sounds, as he wanted to go looking for coons and get them up a tree. Pete also had two beagles, Jack and Queen, for rabbit hunting. Yes, you might say Pete enjoyed hunting and fishing on many a cold winter night.

The couple had fun getting together with their friends by the warm pot-bellied stove, as they enjoyed playing cards. Euchre, their card game of choice, was a lot of fun and helped to pass many a long winter night. Some evenings, Margaret would play the piano while Helen joined in the singing of some pretty familiar songs and would sometimes cry silently. It helped to ease some of the homesick feelings that would come and go while she thought about her family, far way in sunny Florida. Oh how she missed the warm sun and her parents. Sometimes, she would look out into the dark, cold night and see the many bright stars twinkling in the sky.

Helen and Pete made nice friends in Indiana, and usually on Saturday nights, they would go square dancing in the country. The weather was cold and dreary most of the year, and Helen found the discomfort hard to get used to. Spring and then summer with its warm weather was such a welcoming sight. Helen's asthma became very serious, and she could no longer live with the cornfields outside her back window. This was a major problem, causing Helen to return to Florida.

Once again, Pete and Helen attempted to live in Hialeah, where their son Frankie was born on November 30, 1959. It wasn't many years later that Frankie would be able to hit a hole in one and win golf tournaments, golf soon becoming his life's venture. Ann had a brother to play with, and they enjoyed a happy brother–sister relationship.

Sadly, there were many problems in Helen's eight-year marriage. She and Pete kept traveling back and forth between Florida and Indiana, and four different times Helen was able to change jobs from Kent Furniture to National Homes. After ten years and their experiences, both Helen and Pete learned that nothing would ever change. It seemed like it would be better for both parties if Pete returned to the single life he seemed to prefer. As the years past, Pete ignored his children, and Frankie never saw his father again. Happily, Ann would get the opportunity to visit Pete a lifetime later—now, the time would come for a new beginning.

A Sad Good-Bye to Indiana and Hello to Miami, Florida

In 1960, with only the clothes on their backs, Helen, Ann, and Frankie, flew back to Hialeah and stayed with Helen's parents for a few months. This gave Helen time to save enough money to get a small, furnished apartment. Though the children were very young, Frank and Eva were supportive and wonderful. Helen knew taking care of her family on her own wouldn't be easy, but she had faith in God and knew he would guide her and the children in the right direction.

As Helen went about her daily life, she started her mornings by talking and praying to God as she looked in the mirror. Then she would set off to work in her beat-up, old car, hoping it would arrive at her destination. With her strong beliefs, she knew that things would always work out. She was fortunate to have the opportunity to take her very young children to Florida for a much happier environment and to start a new life.

Many days, Ann and Frankie enjoyed the Florida weather dressed in light clothing (shorts and tops) and bare feet. Whenever they could, Frank and Eva took the kids swimming for a fun day at the beach, where they splashed and dashed through the waves. Enjoying quality time with their loving grandparents was a wonderful experience for the children.

After a stressful day at work, Helen would hurry to her mother's home, as the children were waiting. They would happily meet their mother at the door, jumping up and down with excitement, showering her with bear hugs and kisses in a joyful welcome. Eva was a godsend, as she took care of the children for years, allowing Helen to work, and be self-sufficient. After returning from work each evening, Helen had a chance to sit down with her parents and enjoy a cup of coffee with a little snack.

The Statue of Liberty, So Tall and Proud; Her Bright Torch Welcomes the Crowd

Helen worked hard for her family and sometimes would change her job for as little as five dollars more per week. A year later, she would go back to her previous job and ask for another raise in pay. Sometimes it was a little bit scary, as Helen tried to keep things going for her children and herself.

Many times on Saturday afternoons, the small family would park their old, white convertible with holes in the roof in a field near the Miami International Airport. The children would get on top of the hood. It was exciting watching the big jets as they approached and landed on the field. Helen would not have believed that, someday, she would own an airplane and live at a private airport. Living in a place near the rich and famous, including movie stars and racecar drivers, was exciting. It was beyond imagination that it could be possible for anyone to achieve such goals. Was this possible only in America?

Sitting under the Swaying Palms As the Coconuts Drop in Her Arms

As soon as Sundays arrived, Helen and the kids were on their way to Miami Beach to romp in the hot sand; swim in the clear, warm water; and jump like the fishes do, while they tried to beat the oncoming waves. Ann and Frankie would run very fast so as not to burn their tender little feet.

There was a little outside café on the beach where Helen would stop off and chat with some friends. They danced to the outside music, and little Ann and Frankie joined in the dancing. Those were happy days; the small family shared time together and enjoyed their inexpensive outings. Miami Beach was a nice place to bring the children to play and enjoy the waves and fun in the warm sand.

One morning while they were quite young, Ann and Frankie went for a short walk to downtown Hialeah. With only a few nickels in his pocket, Frankie bought a local paper. He proceeded to stand on the street corner, and very soon, a kind man bought his paper for a dime. Frankie had found an easy way to make money, and he kept buying more papers. He was able to double his money. After selling enough papers, Frankie was hungry and wanted to eat. He and Ann were soon off to White Castle to buy some breakfast. This was a new beginning for his promising sales career.

When Ann was about five years old, Helen entered a nice photo of her in a local beauty contest. She won as first runner-up in the Little Miss Hialeah beauty pageant. There was an article in the newspaper, and Ann appeared on Skipper Chuck's TV show. When asked to name her favorite foods, her natural response was "French fries and a hamburger." At only five years old, Ann was a young celebrity. In her teenage years, she took modeling classes and was able to land a few modeling jobs. She also attended dancing school, which she thoroughly enjoyed. Ann was always a lovely well-disciplined young lady, and it was always a pleasure to be in her company. She would long be remembered for her charitable caring for others. She used to save up her weekly allowance of twenty-five cents and add more to her savings to buy her family and friends little gifts at Christmas and birthdays. Later on in life, she would open her own company, Comfort in the Word, and would successfully sell baby quilts with Bible verses.

Life was still difficult, as Helen supported Ann and Frankie on her own. To get back and forth to work, she had to buy a junk car that was always ready for the repair shop. One of her cars was an old convertible with a hole in the roof. The kids liked to tell their mom they had free air-conditioning in their car.

The job market was improving, and Helen became an office manager for a vending company. Things got even better, and she got a new job at Pan American World Airways. The head of industrial engineering and the unit's thirteen industrial engineers needed her, and she worked hard, enjoying every minute and getting the work done in record time. When Helen would leave for California, three women would replace her.

As soon as it was possible, Helen reached her goal to buy a small home. This would allow her and the children to feel safe and have a place to call their own. It was the first of many homes Helen would buy and sell as time went on.

Helen decided to go to school at night at Eastern Airlines to learn to speak Spanish. Many of the Cuban population living in Miami did not speak

English. She was happy to be able to communicate in four languages—
English, Spanish, French, and Ukrainian.

Watching the Water Splash the Boat And the Moon So Bright as They Stayed Afloat

On one of Helen's fun-filled, night owl adventures, she ran into Jay in Miami Springs.

Since Jay was living in Miami at this time, it didn't take very long for him to enter the picture and discover Helen, who would later become the love of his life.

Jay had graduated from Georgia Tech in Atlanta as an industrial engineer. During the Korean War, he'd served as a lieutenant in the air force, as a fighter pilot. He'd remained in the Orient, flying cargo planes. He'd also started his own trading company in Tokyo, Japan, returning five years later to the United States. It wasn't very long before his stepdad invited him to move to Miami to help him out in his Beechcraft aircraft parts business.

Helen and Jay spent many nice evenings sitting on his cabin cruiser at Key Biscayne, and riding along the waves deep into the ocean. Sometimes, the waves were a bit rough, and she felt a bit seasick, causing her to head for the cabin below. The view—as they headed out to sea under the bright moon high in the sky, the boat riding along the splashing, white waves—was an awesome sight.

Helen and Jay enjoyed a lot of fun times, and they looked forward to the holidays and the end of the week. Whenever they could, Jay would take Helen, Ann, and Frankie camping in the Florida Keys. Many times, Frankie was the first and only one to catch the fish. One time, it seemed like a neighbor camper had his eye on Frankie's turtle, and soon Frankie traded the large turtle for the man's fish. It made him feel good to be the top fisherman in the group.

Jay would brave the waterways and take Helen, Ann, and Frankie out on his cabin cruiser. One time, they'd made their way out in the ocean when they somehow hit something. The boat conked out, and they prayed someone would find them. Luckily, God sent a kind fisherman to help them get the boat started, and the kind man gave them a beautiful seashell. It was a very scary time because they were at the mercy of the sea until help arrived.

Helen and Jay enjoyed being together, but Jay was afraid to make the serious commitment of marrying Helen and adopting Ann and Frankie. Over three years, the couple had broken up at least three different times. Jay really loved Helen and the kids, but he thought they would always be there waiting for him. He knew she loved him deeply, but for her, it was time to get serious and settle down. Helen knew she would miss Jay, but she needed a father for her children, and their relationship had to come to an end.

During their last breakup, broken-hearted Helen started dating again. She met Joe, a nice cowboy from Oklahoma. His family was in the oil business, and he was in Hialeah working at the track taking care of thoroughbred racehorses. He was always great to the kids, trying to make a little cowgirl and cowboy out of Ann and Frankie. While out shopping one day, Joe bought them cowboy hats and boots.

After a three-month relationship, Joe was on his way to New York to follow his racehorses. Helen was still on his mind, and Joe made plans for her and the children to join him for a visit in New York. Joe liked the kids and already missed them. He knew that he wanted to marry Helen and adopt her beautiful children.

Shortly after Joe had gone to New York, there were new developments in Helen's life; the phone rang, and on the other end of the line, she heard her old friend, George, from California. He was a designer who had come to Miami eight years earlier to work on a logo for a major airline. He had been thinking about Helen and gave her a call; he wanted to take a short trip to Miami and get reacquainted. Within a few short days of his visit, George rekindled his love for Helen and asked her to be his wife, and move to California with Ann and Frankie. Helen had thought about George over the years and knew that someday, if he came into her life and she was available, they would get married. After eight years, her dream came true.

Ann and Frankie liked George, and they were all in agreement that she would sell her little home in Hialeah and move to California to be with him. She had to give up on her feelings for Jay, since there was no future in their relationship. He was not going to be serious and propose marriage. The time had come to move on with her life and marry George. He wanted to adopt the children, and after so many years, they would have a kind, loving and supportive father.

After George went back home, the phone rang. It was Joe calling from New York; he wanted to make arrangements for Helen and the kids to visit him there. Helen felt sad to talk to Joe and break the news that she had made arrangements to go away to California and get married to a long time friend. Naturally, they were both very upset. Helen was in tears as she hung up the phone. She had enjoyed being with Joe, and they had had many fun times together. But Joe was not the one she would spend the rest of her life with.

She was still crying when the phone rang once again. It was strange to hear Jay's voice on the other end of the line. Almost on cue, after not hearing from Jay for over a three-month period of time, he'd decided to call. He missed her and wanted to make another try at their relationship. Helen talked calmly to Jay and told him she was going to get married and move to California. From her voice, Jay could tell that she had been crying. He told her not to cry or feel bad because Joe would get over his hurt. He wanted to know who she was marrying, anyway. She had told Jay about her dream man from the past who lived in California. It had been eight years since she'd heard from George. She knew he had felt very deeply about their relationship, and he wanted to renew their romance. He would make plans for them to join him as quickly as possible.

Jay wished Helen "good luck," calmly saying good-bye after a very short phone call. There were more tears, and twenty minutes later, Jay was leaning on the doorbell. It was sad to see him looking very unhappy. After the shock had passed, there he was at her front door. Helen was getting married and going to California, and Jay realized that he would no longer be able to see Helen, Ann, and Frankie. He told Helen it was wrong to rush into a serious commitment of marriage, especially to someone else. Even then, Jay was unable to do something about the seriousness of the situation. He was indecisive and felt it was better to do nothing. The following week, before Helen headed to the airport, Jay was on the phone.

He still could not make a commitment, but he was waiting at the airport to wish her good luck He had hoped she would change her mind and not go to California.

Helen's parents hated to see her go so far away. They had just found out that Frank had been diagnosed with lung cancer. But Helen had already made a commitment. The time had come to look for a better life for her and the children. Jay sent Helen a congratulatory telegram in California. Helen and George were married that afternoon.

Within the week, Helen returned to Miami to settle the sale of her home and give notice to leave her job at the airline. Her first evening home, Jay came over with a bottle of champagne to offer his good wishes. He had a special present to give her as a keepsake in memory of the good times and in gratitude for her loving kindness toward him. He wanted her to have one of his treasures he had been keeping, which had belonged to his deceased mother. It was a beautiful, diamond, heart-shaped necklace, which had special meaning. Seeing Jay once again and knowing that he would never be a part of her life was just too much to handle.

Helen knew deep down in her heart that she already missed Jay. She cared for George, who was a wonderful man, but she realized, too late, that her love for Jay ran deep, and he was truly the light in her life. Helen made the difficult decision to leave George and go on alone and suffer in silence.

Her mind made up, she immediately flew back to Los Angeles to tell George in person that she didn't want to hurt him but their marriage was a terrible mistake. She knew that he was a wonderful man and would be understanding. He didn't want them to leave and asked her and the children to stay another week so he could take them all to Disneyland. They went the next day and had a wonderful time, a time they would always remember. It was like a fantasy come true, but Helen's dream had come to an end, and they were soon saying their good-byes to George and California forever. He was a very special man, but it was time to continue life without George and without Jay.

BACK HOME AGAIN TO MIAMI, FLORIDA

Things would be difficult, but Helen had to start all over and put her life back together. She was lucky to get her car back and find a way to save her home. She had sold the home, but there was a glitch in the title work, and the closing was held up. Helen was in luck as the kind man let Helen buy her house back.

Upon her return, she immediately filed for a divorce from George. Meanwhile, Jay heard the good news that she was back. She was surprised when he immediately came over to see her, saying he regretted his actions and the emotional suffering they had both experienced. Helen agreed to marry him after a six-month engagement period. He felt that his stepparents needed to get used to the idea of their forthcoming marriage. A year later Billie, Jay's stepmother, would mentioned to Helen that she was "the best thing that ever happened to our son." There was a new meaning in his life, and he proved to be a wonderful husband and father. Together, Helen and Jay were able to do accomplish a lot.

TRUE LOVE IS REAL AND SHALL LAST FOREVER: EVEN THOUGH THEY TOO SHALL BECOME OLD, SUCH UNDYING LOVE WILL NEVER GROW COLD

On December 14, 1968, Helen happily married Jay, her true love. The wedding ceremony was at the Dade Christian Church, with a small reception at their new home in Country Club, Miami.

Frank and Eva were happy to see Helen settled with a good man like Jay. Frank liked Jay and would always call him Jake. Frank was always happy and liked to kid around. Many times, he was reminded to call him Jay, and he would say, "Okay, Jake."

In March 1969, a bright shining star left our galaxy when Frank passed away at age sixty-nine of lung cancer. He had been ill for only a short time. Friends and family alike would miss his smiling face and the happiness he'd brought to so many.

Jay wanted the best that life had to offer and worked hard to reach his ambitions.
Prior to his and Helen's wedding, he bought a magnificent, new, Mediterranean style home in Country Club, Miami, to share with Helen,

43

Ann, and Frankie. He arranged for three mortgage loans, and with his strong beliefs and careful planning, they were able to make ends meet. He had grown to love Ann and Frankie, and from the very beginning, he considered the family a package deal. He immediately adopted the children, and at last, they were together as a family.

LINDA, SO LIKE THE MEANING IN HER NAME: SHE'S A BEAUTY AND WILL RISE TO FAME

Linda Frances was born on Groundhog Day, February 2, 1970, a bright and shining light almost as beautiful as the stars in the sky. And as each birthday came around, her family enjoyed her more. From the very beginning, she was able to sleep through the night. In the morning, she would wake up smiling, and she'd go to sleep smiling. Sunshine filled the room in her presence. Jay got busy and designed a beautiful bedroom, and each night, he would turn on the intercom to make sure Linda wasn't crying. In a few days, though, the new sleeping arrangement came to an end because Helen and Jay wanted to keep Linda near. Soon, Linda was sleeping in the playpen in the master bedroom alongside their bed. They felt blessed with their new family addition, and Ann and Frankie were pleased to share in her care.

At the time they were married, Jay was working for his stepfather, Ezra, selling aircraft parts. Because Jay had a family to care for, he began to make plans for their future. At this time, Ezra was eagerly trying to sell his parts business and retire. Jay had been a major force in buying and selling the Beechcraft plane inventory of spare parts. He thought this might be a good time for him to buy a percentage of the business. Ezra's plan was to curtail the purchase of future inventory until he was paid in full, and he overpriced his parts business. Sadly, Jay had to turn down his stepfather's offer, as he could not consider such an impossible situation. Then Ezra politely asked Jay to leave, without any notice, since Jay had not agreed to his unreasonable terms.

In order to avoid Ezra and stay out of the aircraft parts business, Jay decided to buy a franchised Burger Castle restaurant. They were going to start working at making some burgers. Of course, their wonderful family got busy and helped in their new restaurant, selling fast-food hamburgers.

They soon became busy, working seven days a week, late into the evening. Even with a day manager, every night was clean-up time, and the family mopped floors till midnight. Within a three-month period, they employed thirteen employees and a day manager; this was not an easy way to make a living for their family. You could almost picture eight-month-old Linda sitting in her highchair next to her momma in front of the cash register. Meanwhile, Helen was busy running back and forth from the cash register to the kitchen and stopping to pay the drivers who were making deliveries at the back door. She was still on the run when she had to put in her orders for chicken in the broiler. Little Linda put on her beautiful smile and just watched and waited patiently as Helen took orders for fries, drinks, and burgers for the people at the counter.

On Fridays and Saturdays many of the help decided to call in sick and stay at home. This was a problem for Helen, as it forced her to come in and work without any notice.

Every morning at 7:00 a.m., the restaurant served coffee and donuts to the telephone company employees who worked across the street. The phone company expected the restaurant to be open to accommodate them. Jay and Helen's restaurant was the latest and newest one to become available in the area. The former owners were from Canada and had a major credit problem. They left many bills unpaid, along with many dissatisfied customers. Jay was determined that the restaurant would make a turnaround and the old customers would return.

The next day, he put his new idea into motion. Helen was the designated driver as the family piled into the car, and Jay led his troops—Ann and Frankie—through the streets of Carol City in Miami. They placed flyers on each and every door in the area. At the doors, they told people that, with the purchase of a hamburger, they would get another one for free. After distributing the flyers, the family returned to the restaurant and found that they were completely sold out—all the hamburgers were gone. Thankfully, some of the nearby restaurants helped out in this dire emergency, selling Jay some of their hamburgers.

Their hard work paid off; the restaurant was able to show a profit in a short three months. Their determination played a big role in their success.

An unfortunate situation arose one day when Jay caught one of the young employees with his hand in the till. He accused the young man of stealing from the cash register and fired him immediately. Helen had to hurry and do payroll for him. An hour later, the young man's father came into the store and attacked Jay, not wanting to believe that his son was guilty of stealing money from the cash register. The police were called, and the young man was in luck because Jay did not press charges

Even though there was a day manager in charge, it was after midnight before the family was able to go home, after mopping floors and working seven days per week. It was difficult to keep up with the public, because many of the people were hard to please. After three months, Jay received an offer on the restaurant. The would-be buyer proposed a small down payment offering to pay the balance within one year. Helen told Jay to make sure he came home with a signed contract. They made an agreement, and Jay was able to sell the restaurant. After working day and night for three months, they were done with their restaurant. Thank you, God, for listening and answering their prayers.

This had been some experience, and they knew there would never be any more fast-food restaurants for them to contend with

Stories That Should Be Told
Continue to Unfold

After the sale of the restaurant, Jay and Helen had to make important decisions for the future. Jay had tried to stay out of the Beechcraft aircraft parts business and wondered what to do next. Their home had three mortgages, and Ann and Frank were in private school. The bills were staggering, and they needed to make a choice. They opened their own company and called it Howington Corporation.

The boys from Brazil, known as Alberto and Alphonso, had an old Beechcraft parts inventory to sell. These parts were not selling and taking up a lot of space in their three warehouses in Hialeah. They knew Jay was an expert in selling aircraft inventory and could help them out. They offered him a chance to broker their inventory of old Beechcraft and SA-16 airplane parts because they believed in his ability to get the job done.

Jay gave it some thought and asked Helen for her opinion. Her response was, "When you need to make money in a hurry, do what you know how to do the best." And that's what they did.

For seventy-five dollars a month, they rented a small room in the front office. The boys from Brazil let them use the warehouse in the rear of the building to work with and store the old Beechcraft parts. Each night, Jay was busy burning the midnight oil, studying bid sales and checking out aircraft parts as they came up for bid. The Boys from Brazil were appreciative and helpful, as Jay worked to sell their Beechcraft and Grumman parts as well.

Helen was eager to help with secretarial work and running the office. She put baby Linda in a playpen in their little one-room office. The area had become unsafe, as many of the nearby businesses were being robbed during the day, and it became necessary to put three locks on the front door with a peephole and a steel gate at the front.

One day when Linda was about three years old and growing fast, Helen looked up from her desk, and there stood little Linda. She had busy little hands that wanted to get into everything, reaching out for the stapler, paperclips, and pencils. Helen put her back in the playpen, but she didn't stay there for long. It was difficult to get any office work done with little Linda on the loose. She was so cute, and it was nice to have her close during the day, but Helen and Jay knew it was time for some changes

Eva saved the day by making a switch—she started watching Linda, and little Jay Jay would stay in the playpen while Momma worked. As the children got older, it became a little easier for Helen to get a lot of work accomplished, as Eva was able to take care of both of the little ones at home. With Frank's assistance, Eva had helped raise all four of Helen's children.

Each day, Jay would call a major company who might be overhauling some planes for foreign countries. The companies would place their orders with Jay, and he would go next door to purchase the needed parts. He, in turn, sold the parts to them for a nice profit. Things were running smoothly, and Jay was beginning to sell the old aircraft parts for the boys from Brazil.

Jay was out of the office one day picking up parts from the overhaul shops in Miami. Without giving any prior notice, an aircraft customer representative surprised Helen by stopping by the office to check on their inventory. She boldly walked with the man next door, showing him a warehouse full of aircraft inventory and pretending the parts were theirs. He was more than pleased to see such a large inventory of parts for their future purchases. Later that day, when Jay returned from his errands he was quite surprised to hear that, once again, Helen had saved the day.

Working tirelessly day and night, Jay and Helen were making enough money to enable Jay to start buying Beechcraft and Grumman parts from secret government bid sales.
They began to stockpile the parts in the garage at home until they could barely close the door. The boxes seemed to fall everywhere whenever the door was opened.

When the Canadian government wanted to sell off their surplus Beechcraft spare parts, Jay secretly bid on them, and the award was for eighteen thousand dollars. Jay got busy on the telephone, selling the parts in advance to many of the Canadian dealers so that he would have enough money to pay for the parts and freight. The inventory included stabilizers, ailerons, wings, generators, and so on. The dealers trusted Jay enough to send thousands of dollars in advance and later picked up their parts in many areas of Canada.
After loading three railroad cars, Jay was forced to leave some valuable inventory behind. At a cost of five thousand dollars, the railroad cars were soon on their way to Hialeah, Florida, in the United States of America.

Jay then had to decide where to store the aircraft parts when they arrived. Helen asked Alphonso to sell him one of the warehouses before the arrival of the aircraft parts. After a bit of negotiating, Alphonso agreed to sell one of his two thousand-square-foot buildings for seventy-five thousand dollars. They almost had a place for the parts that were on their way. But there was a problem. Jay needed to find a place to store Alphonso's old Beechcraft parts. Jay had a great idea; he bought three trailers to store the incoming Beechcraft parts from Canada. When they arrived, he backed the trailers to the front of the building and used them for temporary storage.

During this time, there were numerous visits and phone calls from city officials, including the mayor, demanding the parts' removal. Jay was reminded of the current zoning requirements. Jay ignored their pleas, and three months later the warehouse was emptied. Jay placed the new inventory in the warehouse and removed the trucks from the street. Jay and Helen's garage at home was also emptied of their collection of their own parts, making room for storage of their cars.

This remarkable story of a venture that proved successful from its very beginnings—when some old Beechcraft parts became available—highlights the hard work and determination of an astounding man, Jay, and his family. Sadly, Jay was forced into competition with his stepfather. With very little startup money and very little savings, thanks to help from their immediate family and the kindness of the boys from Brazil, Jay and Helen were successfully able to start and continue their business. Ezra did all he could to hold them back every step of the way, mainly by writing letters to many of the Beechcraft parts buyers all over the world. He told them his son Jay was a broker without any parts of his own and refused to sell him anything. Meanwhile, Jay successfully purchased Grumman parts from secret government bids, as well.

A few years later, the government of France sold their Beech18 parts to a parts broker in California. The broker offered to sell Jay the major portion of the parts. News traveled fast, and Ezra heard about the French inventory. He asked Jay to sell him half of the parts. Jay told his stepdad that the inventory was not for sale, but he would sell him some should the need arise. Very soon, Ezra was buying parts from Jay. The French inventory came to the United States via boat and on to the Miami port. At that time, Jay had the largest Beech 18 parts inventory in the world.

Ezra retired not too long after selling the business to his employee, Al, for a low price. It was sad because Jay had previously taught Al all about the business and would have wanted to keep it in the family. As time went on, Al continued to be nasty and would have no dealings with Jay. Years later, when Ezra was bedridden, he called his stepson, telling him he regretted his actions. He realized that he had treated Jay unjustly and asked for his forgiveness. He wanted Jay to know that he was proud of the whole family and their accomplishments. After shedding a few tears, the pair made up, and Jay's stepdad passed away within a short period of time.

Meanwhile, Frankie was in high school, where he became aware that his ability to sell would be in demand. He began selling boxes of chocolate candy to raise money for his school. It wasn't very long before Frankie's allotment of candy was all gone. Some of the teachers started bringing more boxes of chocolate candy bars that needed to be sold. When the contest was over, he won the highest award for his candy sales. It was nice that he received one hundred dollars as a reward for all his hard work.

When You Arrived, I Knew From the Start You Found A Special Place in My Heart

Little Jay Jay was born prematurely on May 9, 1972, in Miami, Florida. Many times when he would be playing, the house would become very quiet, and he would be nowhere to be seen. That's when Helen would start her frantic search to find him. He would climb up the stairs to his bedroom and lock the door behind him. Helen would bang and bang on the locked door, but there would be no answer. One of these frantic times when everyone was searching for him, luckily someone climbed in the upstairs window and found Jay Jay sleeping in his bed. Sometimes, he would disappear to a corner of the room on the floor. Maybe he needed a little more time to catch up on his sleep, since he had been born five weeks too soon

One time when little Jay Jay was misbehaving, Jay put him in the corner and watched in disbelief as his son threw a temper tantrum, chewing up his little doll. Jay called Helen to come and take a look. She knew Jay Jay was throwing a temper tantrum and remembered the times he would hold his breath until his face turned blue. Jay and Helen quickly learned how to handle his spoiled tantrums.

Jay Jay had the most beautiful blue eyes and a smile that touched your heart. He always seemed so innocent and would quickly turn on the charm. Before long, he too was sleeping in the playpen in their master bedroom alongside Linda. They tried to stretch the days and nights as long as possible to enjoy their wonderful babies. They felt they were blessed, as there were two boys and two girls in the family.

One day a few years later, Linda and Jay Jay asked their parents a surprise question. Ann and Frankie had told them that they had a different father, and the younger siblings wanted to know if that was really true. Ann and Frankie had the same last name as Linda and Jay Jay, as Jay had adopted them a while back, and they never noticed that they were treated any differently. Jay loved all the children and treated them the same; he had, after all, considered the family "his package deal." What a blessing the children were to this family.

One Sunday, while coming home from church, Helen noticed a helicopter and several cars in front of the little white church at the front of the country club entrance in Miami. She told Jay that something big was going on—maybe the president was here to play golf with one of their famous movie-star neighbors. Jay was skeptical, but sure enough, they soon appeared on the scene. Frankie followed them all day, and he could tell you their every move in detail. Even Jacques, their pet poodle, kept getting in the way of their golf game. Everyone liked the famous comedian movie star living in their community, as he was very nice and down-to-earth

So Many Talents Frankie Offers the World As His Great Love for Golf Is Now Unfurled

It was nice to live at Country Club of Miami and have the use of three eighteen-hole golf courses. What a wonderful opportunity for Frankie to play golf, and it became his life's challenge. At about the age of ten, he would practice each day and really enjoyed the game. It wasn't very long before he was carrying golf clubs for the players. Some articles began to appear in golf magazines and newspapers about the powerful swing that this young fellow displayed.

At the dinner table one evening, Frankie mentioned to his father that he had been hitting a hole in one. Jay was proud of Frankie, but he had never hit a hole in one and had to see for himself. They went off to the golf course together, and Frankie hit his hole in one while his dad watched. He was getting to be a young champ and went on to be All-American in high school and a champion player, winning many tournaments and happily collecting trophies. After his graduation, he went on to Miami Dade Junior College on a scholarship and then went on to earn a full scholarship at Centenary College in Louisiana for a year. The college team played in many golf tournaments, and the school plane was always ready to take them to places as far away as Mexico and California. Frankie continued playing professionally, and it was obvious that he loved the game of golf; for many years it became his entire life.

Soon after he and Helen were married, Jay made a wise decision to get a safer sailboat made of fiberglass and equipped with a small motor for family outings. On their next trip, they headed to the Florida Keys. They made camp and hurried off to go sailing in their new boat. With the sounds of thunder in the distance, they could see the ominous clouds above, threatening to rain and ruin their day. Immediately after they set sail, the dark clouds seemed to burst open with a heavy rain, causing a great deal of fear and havoc in their little sailboat. This was their first time out with the sailboat, and they were just learning how to sail; they quickly discovered they had a lot to learn. Sadly, they learned that this was not the time or the place to learn about sailing. It was their good fortune that the Coast Guard quickly appeared on the scene as they fought the waves to stay afloat. The Coast Guard pulled in their little boat with a long rope, and they knew they were lucky to be saved from the raging storm. They were grateful and thanked God for looking out for them and bringing them safely to shore. When they came ashore, Jay was very sick with a bad cold from the freezing rain and quickly searched for a doctor in the Keys. They learned the lesson that, when going sailing, one should always bring along a small motor that could be used in an emergency.

It wasn't very long before they went sailing again to the Florida Keys, renting a small cottage on the water. This time, the sail and boom stayed at home, and they hoped to use their little motor. It was fun and peaceful in the boat as they fished under the hot sun. It was starting to become dark and time to head back to their temporary home. As they made their way toward their little cottage on the water, they seem to have lost their bearings, and Jay was somewhat confused. He kept his cool and told the family not to panic. In their excitement, they lost their oars and would have to use their fishing poles to row back. Jay got off the boat and into the water and started to push the boat. The situation had gotten worse; they could not use the motor, because Jay had forgotten to check on the tides before they set out, and the water was too low and difficult to navigate. Jay, Ann, and Frankie took turns rowing, dipping their fishing poles into the water, where there might be sharks lurking below. Then they would bravely jump in, taking turns pushing the boat all the way to their rented cottage. In all the excitement, Ann dropped her glasses in the ocean, causing her a lot of difficulty seeing. After many scary moments, they made it to the little cottage. They may have had a lot of frightening moments, but they would tell you it was a lot of fun and would do it all over again.

The family enjoyed visiting Aunt Lena in St. Petersburg, as she lived across the street from the beach. They would gather seashells in the white sand and swim on the tropical beach. After Aunt Lena passed on, her niece, who lived in Alabama, inherited the beach cottage. Since Lena's niece was unable to maintain the older home, Helen and Jay bought the cottage from her. On many weekends, they would drive up from Miami to remodel the little cottage. One time, Jay folded up his little motorcycle and put it in his plane and was soon off to St. Pete Beach to do some needed repairs on the little cottage. When he parked the plane at the airport, he took out his little Italian motorcycle and headed for the beach. It wasn't very long when, lo and behold, Nancy's husband Eddie was honking the horn at Jay. He was very surprised to meet his brother-in-law unexpectedly in St. Petersburg.

After spending a lot of time working on the cottage, Jay and Helen decided to sell it, and Helen was able to quickly market the cottage over the phone.

STORIES THAT NEED TO BE TOLD
CONTINUE TO UNFOLD

Jay had mentioned to Helen how good his ex-wife was at selling real estate, but she had ruined him financially, taking all of his assets within a six-month period. Helen was the love of his life, and his experience with his ex-wife may have been the reason he was afraid to make a commitment. He suggested that it would be a very good idea for Helen to study real estate and work at home. Upon his wise advice, she took a real estate course at the local high school at night at a cost of two dollars. Helen was pregnant with Linda at the time, and she took her real estate exam in Ft.

Lauderdale. With Linda's assistance and strong kicking in her stomach, she passed the exam.

It was time to begin her real estate sales career, and from the very beginning she was very successful. Jay would help her with excellent sales advice, and remarkably, she was able to sell expensive homes and land in her home area. When Grandma Eva was not available, little Linda had to go with Helen on her sales calls. Most times, Helen found it easier to go to open houses with Linda on her hip. Helen and the baby would be selling real estate together.

In the beginning, Helen worked for several other real estate brokers, and after a year, she became a broker herself. She worked very hard after opening her own office called Town and Country Realty of Miami. Within two years, she became well known, as she listed and sold many homes in the nearby area. Since Helen had proven to Jay that she was very successful in her real estate sales, it wasn't necessary to hear anymore about Jay's ex-wife. All along, he really knew there would never be any comparisons to the two women and was more than happy to call Helen his "money machine."

After Helen's first year in real estate, she went up to New Smyrna Beach and bought a small island of ten acres on Williams Road and Turnbull Bay. For five years, Helen would pay for this property out of her commissions. Jay said that if she bought the property on time payments, he would be sure to back her up. They would get excited about the property, and each year they would take a ride to the New Smyrna-Daytona area. Many years later the property would be surveyed, split in two, and sold. Today, it can be found in the deed records as Howington Subdivision.

As Jay and Helen drove up Old Pioneer Trail to check on their little island, they noticed a small sign: "Airport". It seemed interesting; excitedly, they followed the sign up along the dirt road to the back gate of Spruce Creek Fly-In.

Spruce Creek had formerly been an old navy base and was in the process of being developed into a fly-in community, including a country club and golf course. The development was just about to get off the ground, and sales of lots would soon begin. As the properties became available, Jay and

Helen were the first to buy a commercial acre for their business, along with a large, wooded taxiway lot to build their dream home and airplane hangar. It was wonderful to know that they found their way through the back gate and came out with the prize. Luckily, they had bought some good properties at unheard of low prices. Jay had hoped to continue his aircraft business at the airport. Little did they know that Spruce Creek would become the biggest private airport in the world and the home of many famous people, affording Helen a golden opportunity to assist the new residents in the purchase and sale of their properties.

While living in Miami, Jay confessed to Helen that he had been dreaming about airplanes with a great desire to begin flying, once again. He bought a twin Beech18 airplane and kept it parked at the airstrip near the entrance at Country Club of Miami. Twenty years had passed since he was in the cockpit of a plane, and he felt he needed some lessons in flying to get his license current. Jay's interest in flying increased, and he decided to sell the Beech 18 airplane and buy a Cessna 310 for his busy flying days ahead.

Helen's priest from the Russian Greek Orthodox Church came out to the flying field at Spruce Creek for prayers and God's blessings over the couple's new plane.

Later, Jay's long time dream of flying helicopters became a reality when he took flying lessons using his GI bill. Each afternoon as Jay was taking his flying lessons, he would fly over their home. The noise was deafening, and it wasn't very long before some of the neighbors were on the phone to complain. Helen knew it was time to make a quick run in the car to the corner runway to meet the helicopter. They both looked forward to their daily practice ride in the rented plane. Helen climbed aboard the helicopter with Jay, and together they enjoyed the panoramic view below. It seemed like they were right on top of the cows in the field. It was fun to share the excitement of the ride and do some crazy things in their daily adventures. Of course, Jay passed his test, got his license, and would be able to fly helicopters whenever he had time. He was a daring pilot and sometimes reminded Helen of the *Terry and the Pirates* comic strip.

On their way to Maine to visit some friends, Jay and Helen ran into a lot of unexpected bad weather; the plane shook, and the experience was somewhat scary. As a professional pilot, Jay knew what to do in case of an emergency, and he immediately turned the plane back toward Atlantic City, New Jersey. As the Cessna landed, a nice, young chauffer approached the plane and asked if they were the Rockwells. Helen politely told him that they were the Howingtons. It wasn't moments until the skies opened up, with loud claps of thunder and streaks of lightning that lit up the skies. After they waited out the storm, Jay and Helen were, once again, on their way, soaring above the majestic clouds.

Another time, they flew to New York City to visit their family. Flying into New Jersey in the dark of night, they attempted to land at a small airport. Jay tried to come in for a landing but was unable to do so. The landing lights on the field would not stay on long enough for the plane to make a safe landing, and with a quick response, Jay immediately pulled the plane up. They needed landing lights to make a landing. In the dead of night, they began their search for another landing field. Knowing they were lost, they decided to continue circling over the skies for another twenty minutes. Looking below, Jay spotted a small airport a few miles farther away and proceeded to land at the airport. They were supposed to meet up with Helen's sister, Anna, and her husband, John, at the Old Bridge Airport. Instead, they made it to another airport eight miles away where they saw a diner on the field with several policemen drinking coffee on their break. Two of the policemen left Helen and Jay at the café while they went off to find Anna and John, who were worried and glad to hear of their safe arrival. They decided to leave the plane parked at the private airport and drove home with Anna and John instead.

When they returned to New Jersey from Long Island after visiting Nancy and Eddie, Tina and Walt, and Mary and Joe had some difficulties with the plane's starter. After they left and were on the busy highway in the sky, Jay mentioned that he'd had some difficulty getting the plane started, and after using some tools, they were soon on their way. He told Helen not to worry as he would replace the starter when they landed in New Jersey, and once the plane had started everything would be okay. It was exciting to see New York City from above as planes of all sizes were flying in every direction and getting too close. Looking down below, they could see the city lit up like a Christmas tree with bright lights everywhere, and sometimes the planes were under them and then above them. Their airplane seemed to be approaching the fast lane on the highway to heaven.

There were many exciting moments for the whole family during their flying times. Helen was a bit nervous up in the sky and would count on her faith, always taking her Bible along for the ride, and a tranquilizer.

For twenty years Jay had had many dreams of flying, and they had finally come true. Later on after the family relocated to Daytona, he would enjoy flying back and forth from Miami to Daytona.

On to Daytona: Near the World-famous Beach

A few years later, Helen noticed a big change in the area of Hialeah and Miami. Many Cuban refugees had escaped from Cuba to be free and had settled there. It was known as Little Havana. The people were very nice and worked very hard. Spanish was often the language of choice, as the new settlers spoke to each other in their native tongue. At times, Helen and Jay felt like strangers in their own country.

They were successfully handling their business affairs, but it was evident that it was time to make a new start at Spruce Creek Airport in Daytona. Frankie wanted to stay in Miami, as he was working toward a golf scholarship, and the family arranged for him to stay with his lady golf coach to finish out his senior year. Ann decided to stay in Hialeah in her little condo, as she had a good job at one of the airlines. Helen knew it would be difficult for Grandma to give up her little home in Hialeah. She planned to move in with Helen and the troops, while both houses were being sold. Helen did sell the home at once, and with a bit of sadness, Eva gave up her home that she shared with Frank for over ten very happy years.

A few months before they moved to Daytona, Eva found a lost baby bird and named him Sam. Each day, she would let him go free into the trees behind the screened pool. Sam would always come home when she called him. A few days before moving day, Sam acted strange and did not want to come home when she called, but he came anyway.

At last, Helen sold their home in Country Club of Miami and thought about the happy times. The house had provided them shelter and had been their home for over ten years. It had seen the births of Linda and Jay Jay.

After packing up their dog; Sam, the bird; two ducks, Daisy and Charlie; and the goldfish the family was on the way to Daytona.

Upon their arrival, they rented a nice two-story home on the taxiway at Spruce Creek on Lazy Eight Drive. While they were unloading the moving van, they received a phone call. The buyers were advising that they were unable to close on the sale; a company had offered the buyers such a good deal that they'd broken the contract. They allowed Jay and Helen to keep their deposit. Helen promptly ran an ad for the weekend, sending Jay to Miami to show the home. They needed a quick sale, and Jay the super-salesman sold the home to the first buyer that answered the ad.

From their porch, they could view the airplanes coming and going down Lindy Loop as they taxied home to their hangars. Since Jay was not quite ready to leave the business in Miami, he commuted in their Cessna 310 for three years, landing the plane in their back yard. Little Jay Jay loved to stand in front of the plane and feel the strong wind as they all pushed the plane into the hangar. Jay enjoyed his flying trips back and forth between Daytona and Miami.

The family enjoyed playing with Sam, the bird, as he would bounce a ball back and forth on the pavement. A few weeks after their arrival, though, Sam seemed lonesome and climbed the tallest tree that was nearby. They could see him as he said good-bye. Eva told them, "Look, he won't be back. He's heading back to Hialeah."

She had become fond of Sam, and she thought about him for many weeks later. They were sure he'd find his way back, as he was a strong bird.

Eva also had two ducks named Charlie (a handsome Mallard) and Daisy (a white Muscovy). They were Grandma's pets. She made a small fence outside the living room window, so she could watch over them. The family watched Daisy from the window as she sat on her baby eggs and were saddened when, each day, a snake would come and steal one of the eggs. Both Charlie and Rosie were afraid of the snake, causing Daisy to move away as another egg was taken away. It was sad to watch the eggs as they disappeared each day, but nature always seemed to have a way to take care of life's creatures.

Looks Like Charlie Has Found a New Friend: Hoping They'll Stay Together Till the End

At daybreak one morning, Charlie made such a commotion that it woke up Eva and Helen. They rushed down the stairs to see why Charlie was quacking very loudly and flying about. As he saw they were following him for the first time, he sped up; they could see him ahead, flying through the trees at great speed. Eva and Helen ran as fast as their legs would carry them to keep up with Charlie, who was leading them to the nearby lake. Sadly, they found some white feathers along the ground, leading to Daisy. She had been chased and bitten by a wild dog, and they found her dead, lying on the ground. All the while, Charlie quacked, crying in despair as he saw Daisy lying still on the ground. They, too, were saddened by what they saw, and they promptly buried Daisy. Eva carried her saddened Charlie home, and she could tell he was crying all the way.

As each day passed, Charlie sat quietly thinking about his Daisy and how he missed her. He would not eat, even though Eva tried talking to him. She felt bad for Charlie, and within a week, she went out to buy a duck for him. Mike at a nearby gas station sent Eva to his friend's farm, where she bought another duck named Rosie. Charlie and Rosie made a good pair, and the two ducks were happy together, as Charlie took to her at once. The ducks and the whole family were happy.

Listen to the Wedding Bells as They Ring Almost Makes Me Want to Get up and Sing

Ann worked at a clothing store in Miami, where she met Bruce. There was something special in the air, and soon they fell in love. She knew he was the man of her dreams, and after a short courtship, they were married on February 20, 1983, in Coral Gables, Miami, and a small reception followed. Their three beautiful children are Jordan Alexander, Lauren Anastasia, and Wyatt Andrew.

A year later, Helen and Jay bought a ranch home on the creek with two and a half acres in "A Quiet Place in the Country," which is a subdivision in a rural area near Spruce Creek. This was a small ranch community with room for horses. It was peaceful and quiet at their new home, and they were able to park their Cessna at the surrounding airport in Spruce Creek. Jay was not ready to settle down. When he would return to Daytona, he would fly directly over the house and let Helen know it was time to drive over to Spruce Creek and get the car and bring him home.

Three years later, Helen informed Jay that it was time to settle down, sell the building in Miami, and move the aircraft parts to their little airport in Daytona Beach. Helen sold the Hialeah warehouse immediately over the phone. At long, long last their parts were headed to Daytona Beach. They were able to build a 9,000-square-foot airplane hangar on Cessna Boulevard at Spruce Creek, and the parts arrived shortly from Miami.

Helen opened her new realty company, Spruce Creek Realty, and it didn't take long for her to sell over one hundred lots and homes at A Quiet Place in the Country. Many of the lots were sold on the "no down payment plan."

Spruce Creek Fly-In was a very unique development and was known as the world's largest fly-in development, housing over five hundred airplanes on over fifteen hundred acres. Included were many large jets in a guarded community, with a country club and golf course and a paved and lighted private airport. It took a bit of work and several years before it became known as the largest private airport in the world. It did take some convincing, but people settled there from many different countries. A few years later, Helen was able to build her new building, the Spruce Creek Corporate Center on Cessna Boulevard. This was the commercial area, where many other businesses were to follow. Helen rented offices in the building and used the other half for her realty services.

Helen and Jay were happy to be in Spruce Creek and far away from their hectic days in Miami. Jay would be able to sell aircraft parts out of his new warehouse on Cessna Boulevard as well. Helen was in the realty business, and this afforded her an opportunity to buy real estate at the best prices. It was a lot of hard work, but it was always nice to help people in their real estate choices.

Eva's role as grandma was special, as she helped the family in many ways, and they were happy she chose to move to Daytona and live with them. There were many times Linda would get in trouble with her dad. He'd want to punish her, but she'd make a mad dash to her grandma's room, locking the door behind her. Linda was safe in the room, hiding behind the door, with Grandma rushing to her defense. It's easy to laugh about the situation now, but at the time, it may have made her dad a little bit angry.

Since Grandma was home during the day and everyone had things to do, the family needed to find something that would keep her happy and busy. The TV was the next best answer, starting with the soap opera *General Hospital*. Eva really enjoyed the story, and before long she'd become invested in three soap operas. She did not want to be disturbed while she watched her stories, as she sat comfortably with the dog, Dusty. He kept watch next to the TV, and it was hard to get near her for kisses.

The sisters, Mary, Tina, Anna, and Nancy, moved to Daytona to be near the family. Several times a week, Tina started to came over to sit with Mom. Then each afternoon or in the evening, Mary and Joe, Nancy and Ed, and Anna and John would come over to play some cards, tell old stories, and drink coffee. Jay always welcomed the family.

Sometimes Eva would get out her harmonica and entertain everyone with pretty songs. One song she loved to play was "You Are My Sunshine." She enjoyed her grown children visiting with the family and was always in a happy mood. Jay enjoyed the company and entertained the family as well. He remembered his life was sometimes lonely growing up as an only child. Sometimes when the family would meet, he would take the whole group out and treat them to ice cream. They had lived far away for many years, and they finally were able to spend more time together and be close.

One fine day, Jay Jay was fishing with his mother in the backyard on the creek, and he was somewhat impatient that the fish weren't biting. He turned around and told her to sit right there, and he would be right back. Stepping aside, he said a short prayer and then continued to fish. "Ask and ye shall receive," and that's what he did. After catching some fish, Jay Jay threw them back in for another day of fishing. They spent some quiet times fishing on the little creek behind their home. Jay Jay was strong in his faith in the Lord.

Later, Jay Jay would enjoy working on commercial charter boats, as they fished out in the deep water. When the fish were on, he hauled in a bunch of fresh fish and sold some to the nearby restaurants.

During his teen years, Jay Jay liked to play near the covered bridge in A Quiet Place in the Country. One afternoon while he was climbing over a tall tree that leaned over the creek, something unusual happened—he lost his footing. He started to pray as he began to fall, landing in the arms of a branch. He knew it was a long, perilous way down, and the fall could have ended in sheer disaster. But he truly believed the hand of God had prevented him from hitting the bottom. He knew that the power of prayer and his strong belief in the Lord was with him that day.

Jay and Helen began to plan and design their new home at Spruce Creek. At a young age, Jay knew that he had always wanted to be a builder and create beautiful homes. Soon the work was underway, and Jay went to Daytona Beach Community College to study architecture and design. He worked up a complete set of drawings; the home to be built in the French Country style. The building plans were a bit complicated. The house featured four bedrooms, five bathrooms, a sauna, and a stylish breezeway leading to an airplane hangar. It included a seven-foot water wheel powered by water or electricity with the turn of the electric switch.

Jay worked every day for almost three years overseeing the construction of their royal home. It was like a castle, with a brick turret in the front and a large water wheel. Unfortunately, during the construction of their home at #2 Lazy Eight Drive, Jay suffered a massive bleeding stroke to the brain. Only fifty-seven years of age, he was paralyzed on the left side. It became necessary to hire a builder to finish the project.

When Jay came home from the hospital, they were able to carry him upstairs and downstairs to see the completion of the finished product—a work of art. After the tour was finished, Jay's eyes welled up with tears, and he cried with happiness. The home was completed, and his hospital bed was in the busy family room. He could look through the glass doors and watch the planes as they taxied along Lindy Loop. It was sad that he could not fly them anymore. Most days, Tina would tie him up in his wheelchair and take him for long walks to enjoy the sights. They would watch the activities at the airport in the warm Florida weather. Tina was wonderful, and she came six days a week to care for Jay. He was always able to joke and make everyone laugh, though he was bedridden and totally dependent on Helen and Tina.

One day, Helen coaxed Jay to pick up his paralyzed leg for a big kiss. He did so one hundred times, as she gave him one hundred kisses. Sadly, he could never move his leg or walk again, although he tried. With a big smile on his face, Jay reminded Helen, "I expect to be taken care of in the manner I am accustomed to." This went on for over a period of five years, and he was taken care of as he wished, while the family showed him a lot of patience and love. It was good to have him home.

Helen reminded Jay that she used to ask him to get home on time to enjoy his family at the dinner table. Because he could not eat or swallow his food anymore and was kept alive by a stomach tube, he would be sure to be home on time. Life was difficult during those five years, but Jay always had a great sense of humor. He could still make everyone laugh, despite his stroke and brain damage. Shortly thereafter, Jay's teacher and classmates took a class trip to see Jay's finished work and the completion of the home. As the group went from room to room, you could see the expressions of pleasure on their faces. Jay, too, was proud to show what determination and hard work could accomplish.

It was no surprise when *The News Journal* printed a full-page story with some pictures of their unique home. Here was the proof that dreams can become real.

Helen continued her busy real estate business close to home, which enabled her to be nearby for Jay while taking care of the family. Grandma Eva was there to help out. Linda and Jay Jay would also tend to their father as needed. There was deep affection for Jay and a lot of love in their home on Lazy Eight Drive.

Helen brought a beautiful Macaw parrot home. Captain was the star of the pet shop and could talk like a little child. He liked to scream and carry on very loudly when he wanted attention. When Helen was at home, she spent a great deal of time sitting and caring for Jay. Since Captain was also in the family room with Jay, he became jealous and wanted all of Helen's time. He let her know by shrieking loudly for attention. Jay was trapped in the room and was forced to listen to the loud noise. With a funny grin on his face, he would yell out, "Shoot the damn bird." Jay was frail, and while taking care of him may have been a lot of work, the family was glad to have him around for a while longer.

Sometimes when Captain was out of his cage, Dusty would charge right after Captain. It didn't take long for Captain to return the favor and go after the dog. The sight of Dusty back away from the bird until he was safe and out of sight was endearing. Months later, Helen knew Jay needed some peace and quiet, and sadly, she found a new home for Captain with her friend, Jackie. The home had become quiet, and everyone missed Captain, the talking bird. When she could, Helen would visit Captain at Jackie's, and she was relieved to see that he was happy and had a new friend in the next cage.

The doctors felt that Jay might live for two years in his frail condition. He desperately wanted to be a part of the family, even though it was difficult for him to do so. It was amazing that he stayed around for five years and watched the children grow into their teens. It was a proud day when Linda graduated from Spruce Creek High School, and her dad was in attendance in his wheelchair.

For holiday fun, the extended family would come over, and they would enjoy dinner together. Helen would ask Jay if he wanted to sit at the table with everyone while they ate. With that funny little grin on his face, he always said he wanted to join the family. He never wanted to miss anything. Jay could join in conversation and watch the family eating the good food on the table. After everyone went home, Helen would go to the refrigerator. She would heat the mashed potatoes and a bit of stuffing and gravy. Very carefully, she would spoon it out to Jay, one swallow at a time. She knew how much he enjoyed the family holiday dinners and asked him not to tell anyone that she fed him by mouth, especially Tina. Sure enough, the next morning Jay could hardly wait to report to Tina about his mashed potatoes, gravy, and turkey stuffing. Oh, well, Helen said, they would worry about that at the next holiday dinner.

One day, Tina and Helen took Jay to the doctor for a visit .The waiting room was full of people, and Helen had to sit across the room. While Jay was sitting across the room in his wheelchair, he spotted Helen. In a very loud voice, he yelled across the room, "Helen, I love you."

It was a beautiful gesture, and Helen yelled back, "I love you too."

True Love is Real and Will Last Forever: Even Though They too Shall Become Old, Their Undying Love Will Never Grow Cold

May 28, 1989, was a sad day for the family and for many friends, as Jay quietly went to sleep to be with the Lord. Helen and Jay were married for twenty years and wished for still a little more time. It was going to be difficult to go into the empty family room each morning to greet Jay and find an empty hospital bed with Jay gone. For five years, that dear man had never complained, though he'd suffered greatly, and had brought tears of laughter to the family's eyes.

The family suffered a deep emptiness with the loss of a wonderful husband and loving father. His illness and suffering would be no more. They would miss his funny ways and *Terry and the Pirates* excitement and the love and joy he shared with those near him. The light of their life had left for a better place, and they were sure that he was laughing with the angels on high, who were enjoying his great sense of humor. Jay's family—Ann, Frankie, Linda, Jay Jay, and Helen would always be his package deal, always sharing in his love.

Jay liked to put things off to the last minute, causing him to be late many times. As a joke, Helen would kid him and tell him he would surely be late for his own funeral. Well, her prediction came true. Ann was living in Miami and had to catch a plane to Daytona. The funeral service was held up as they waited for more than an hour because Ann's plane from Orlando was delayed. The funeral director kept coming into the room requesting to have the service without her in attendance. Upon her arrival, they began the funeral service. Who knew that it would come true and Jay would be late for his own funeral. They all did!

Shortly after Jay's death, the Victory Baptist Church had a special memorial service and planted a camphor tree in the front yard of the church on Taylor Road.

Many times while Jay was alive he had talked about religion and heaven, always keeping his faith. Helen told Jay that he would go to heaven, and somehow she would someday show him that she was right again. He would just nod his head and smile.

The morning after Jay passed away, something very strange happened. Helen had the most realistic dream that she was talking to Jay. He wanted to let her know that she was right again, and he was happily on his way to heaven. He didn't want to leave without saying good-bye. She was awakened by a rush of warmth through her whole body and jumped right out of bed. She was reassured that Jay was on his way and would meet her someday in that beautiful place known as heaven. Miracles do happen, and it was the family's good fortune to have Jay in their lives. His presence made such a difference in the time they shared together.

JAY JAY NEEDED TO THINK AND GET AWAY: A HURRIED SEARCH WAS SOON UNDERWAY

One evening in 1989, Jay Jay decided to run away from home at Spruce Creek, as he wanted to be alone and needed some time to think.

It was getting late, and darkness had set in. Jay Jay had not come home for dinner, and there was no sign of him anywhere. Helen searched the house and drove around the streets of Spruce Creek for a long time, calling for him. She was worried that he might be lost, cold, and hungry. Where could he be?

Leaving a short note on top of his bed, Jay Jay didn't think he'd be missed for a while, and if so, hoped that his mother wouldn't worry. Helen was quick to imagine wild thoughts when she did not see the note on the bed in his room.

Jay Jay rode his bicycle over to "A Quiet Place in the Country" and stayed under the covered bridge for several hours into the late evening, searching for some peace and quiet. It was late, and he missed his safe, warm bed as he began to get cold and hungry. He had had enough excitement getting away from home and sitting under the covered bridge with the mosquitoes. He missed his family and decided to head home to his family and safe, warm bed. When he walked in the door, Helen, Linda, and Grandma Eva cried with happiness to see him safely back home again. He said that he had taken his Bible with him and had left his mom a note on the bed telling her not to worry. Jay Jay had come home; their fears were gone, and their prayers had been answered.

In the summer of 1989, shortly after Jay had passed on, Linda, Jay Jay, and Helen enjoyed a short cruise to St. Thomas and the Virgin Islands. Many of the sights proved different and interesting, and they enjoyed great food and entertainment aboard ship. Linda and Jay Jay made many new friends staying up very late each night. At about 10:00 p.m. each evening, they eagerly escorted their mother safely to their cabin. They were free to roam the ship and dance the night away with their new friends. When morning arrived, they were unable to get out of bed and slept until noon. Helen was on her own as she headed to the dining room for a tasty breakfast. They all felt safe on the ship and were able to relax.

It's Wonderful that Mothers Become Grandmothers: They are so special, this We Know Like No Others

A time for sadness had reached Helen's home once again. Her wonderful Momma, Grandma her children loved, Eva had to leave them, bound for heaven. She was eighty-six years old and in good health, but the doctors were fearful that she might have a stroke. She needed an operation as the arteries in her neck had become blocked. The operation was successful, but a blood clot came loose, causing a stroke. She died peacefully in her sleep on January 6, 1990, during the Russian Christmas holiday.

During the fifteen years she lived with Helen's family, she had showered them with a special love. She would be missed, as would her harmonica music and singing. Each morning, Helen would wake up to the delicious aroma of fresh coffee and her momma's smile waiting downstairs. Eva and Helen had shared wonderful moments and pleasant talks to start off each day. Though, she was extremely busy, Helen would make time to listen to Eva's stories about her life's interesting adventures. When Helen was young, it was nice to know that when she was frightened, Eva would hold her in her arms and tell her not to cry or worry. She said everything would turn out all right, and it usually did. Today, Helen tells her own children and grandchildren the same thing. It helps to think back to Eva's famous words of comfort and share them with the children and grandchildren.

Colorado on Top of the Mountains They Go In Summertime with Rooftops Full of Snow

In August 1990, it was time for a getaway, and Linda, Jay Jay, and Helen flew off to Denver, Colorado. The ten-day trip mainly consisted of traveling throughout the state. David, a friend in real estate, offered his beautiful three-story mansion for their stay up in the Genessee Mountains in Golden, Colorado, with breathtaking views of Mt. Evans. David's secretary was at the airport waiting for their arrival and helped them to get settled for their stay.

It wasn't very long before David met up with them, quickly driving them around. First thing on the agenda was to climb Gray's Peak. It was an awesome sight to look at the heavy snow piled on top of the mountains in the summer. As soon as Helen heard the thunder and saw the lightening, she was terrified, as the lightning seemed to appear next to her, lighting up the sky. In sheer terror, Helen ran down the mountain to the car as fast as her legs could carry her. Jay Jay and Linda were brave and continued to climb farther up the mountain with Dave. They didn't let the dangerous lightning affect their excitement.

Jay Jay and Linda did not fear the storm as they kept on climbing farther up the mountain with their new friend. Helen bravely sat alone in the car, terribly frightened by the storm and shaking in her boots. It seemed like forever, but within an hour Dave and the children, a little out of breath, came down the mountain and joined her. Their cheeks were rosy red and they had satisfied looks on their faces. After a short rest, they had stopped to gather some of the colorful wildflowers. Upon their return to the car, they sheepishly handed the flowers to their mother, who was anxiously waiting.

The air was very dry, and it would be easy to see how the hand and body lotion business would be booming all over Colorado. At such high elevation, you almost feel like you are on top of the world. It's possible that this was why our country is called "America the Beautiful."

Dave was nice enough to let Helen and the kids borrow his four-wheel drive to visit the scenic wonders in and around Colorado. Looking down the snow-covered mountains, they could see the natural waterfalls spilling over the landscape, with gigantic rock formations painting a picture of true natural beauty. As they rode over the picturesque mountains on the Silverton train to Durango, they made a short stop to explore a gold mine. It was a special time, as Helen thought about the past and her dad going to work each day in a dark, damp coal mine in Pennsylvania.

On day two, they went to Red Rocks Park, where the red rocks scenery was breathtaking, and then on to the Coors Beer Plant in Golden. They enjoyed the beer-tasting experience as they discovered how beer was made. Early the next morning, they were on their way to Vail, up a steep mountain for some interesting sights. They made a short stop at Idaho Springs for white water rafting on the Colorado River. Rafting down the cold river was a bit scary, and they could see mountains of reds, purples, grays, browns, and greenery, with snow-capped tops. Near the latter part of the boat ride, the navigator stopped the boat and let the group put their hands in the steaming water, where the smell of sulfur was very strong.

On the way to Aspen, Helen and the kids passed through San Isabel National Forest. Then they were off to the White River National Forest, which was also picturesque.
On the next day, Dave took Helen to downtown Denver to show her some of the homes and business complexes he had built and developed. It felt a bit strange as they drove past the freight yards, looking for the slaughterhouse thinking back to times of the wild west days when they brought in the cows for slaughter.

Meanwhile, Jay Jay and Linda kept busy by going fishing for the day. Since Jay Jay was unable to catch a fish on his line, he decided to pick up someone's dried-up, old, dead fish and took a picture. It smelled like an old fisherman's tale.

Frank & Eva
Sometime Ago

Southern Poland many years ago

SOMETIME IN 1940

NANCY, ANNA, TINA, JOHN, AND HELEN

EVA, FRANK AND SPOTTY
1955 IN FLORIDA

Our Cessna-310

John Christopher Howington, Sr.
(J.C.) in Air Force

WEDDING DAY IN 1983
ANN AND BRUCE

GRANDCHILDREN
WYATT, LAUREN, MOM
ANN, JORDAN - 2010

FRANKIE -2009

JOHN C., AYDEN, MOGUL (DOG), JAY JAY, LOGAN IN YEAR 2008

WEDDING DAY
JAY JAY AND CARRIE

HELEN AND DAUGHTER ANN
IN THE YEAR 1977

HELEN AND SON FRANKIE
DAYTONA, 2009

GRANDCHILDREN
LOGAN, EMMA, JOHN
AND AYDEN IN 2010

LINDA AND JAY JAY
IN YEAR 1992

WEDDING DAY IN 2000
LINDA AND PETE

FRANKIE, HELEN, LINDA
AND JAY JAY IN 2007

THE GIRLS IN JULY 15, 2000

ANNA HELEN NANCY MARY TINA

1992
Linda, Ann, Helen, Frankie
& Jay Jay Howington

The next day, the trio visited Central City and the City of Black Hawk, with an elevation of 8,042 feet, and made a short stop to explore an abandoned mine. They visited the Lost Gold Mine. It was creepy, dark, narrow, and steep, and they found some fool's gold in an abandoned mine shaft. Again, Helen thought about her father and how he might have felt working in the dangerous coal mines.

The highlight of their trip was the Silverton-Durango all-day train ride, where they enjoyed looking at the picturesque mountain streams from high elevations riding through the mountain passes. They found the ride to be very dangerous, as the mountains were steep with very few guardrails for protection at such high elevations.

Driving to the southwesternmost tip of the state, they were able to stand on the top of the mountain and see a panoramic view of Utah to the west and Arizona and New Mexico to the south. As they were in Colorado, it was amazing to see four states at the same time.

When Jay Jay got up each morning, he was always looking out the window for a glimpse of the wild deer that might be nearby in the wooded area surrounding the house. As they were preparing to leave on their last morning stay, as luck would have it, a family of deer approached him as they came out of the woods to forage for food. Jay Jay was excited, and he ran into the house and called everyone to come quickly to see the deer in Dave's backyard. He took pictures while watching the deer, who seemed unafraid and remained up close and out in the open.

Upon leaving, Helen and the kids thanked their kind friend, Dave, for making their summer trip enjoyable and possible. On the way home to Daytona Beach, they thought they might miss Colorado and the majestic mountains, unbelievable sights, and especially the snowball fights in the summer.

Helen Needed Time to Rest, As
She Gave Up all that Stress
Riding to London, Venice, and
Rome on the Orient Express

In November 1990, Helen's friend, Margaret, from England thought it might be time to recharge their batteries and asked Helen to join her on a trip to Europe to visit England, Venice, and Rome. Margaret made all the arrangements, and the pair was off on a new adventure, to enjoy an exciting train ride on the mysterious Orient Express.

The Magical City of London

Upon arrival at Gatwick Airport, Helen and Margaret took the British railroad train as they headed for the Mountbattten Hotel in London, where they enjoyed the famous sights and sounds of the world famous city of London.

Walking along, they stopped at Covent Garden and visited a small café, situated below the street level, to enjoy hot coffee and cakes. It was reminiscent of a café they had seen in a French movie. As they moved along, they soon heard the sounds of laughter and noticed a number of people sitting around at a large market square. Immediately, Helen became interested in watching "Charlie" doing his Charlie Chaplin routine. She soon realized that he was pointing his finger toward her, inviting her to join his routine. This was something to write home about, as she was soon balancing him up in the air with his weight upon her legs and shoulders. During this time, Margaret was busy taking pictures. He did not speak before or after the show, though Helen tried to get him to talk. A year later, he would send Helen a postcard from Switzerland, where he was appearing.

After a bit of freshening up, Helen and Margaret were on the go again. After a tasty dinner at their grand hotel, the Mountbatten, they headed to a theater where they watched a play called *Love Letters*, starring an American movie star, George Peppard. They enjoyed the play, though it was sad and made Helen cry. It was a very cold and damp night as they waited outside the stage door, hoping for a glimpse of the handsome movie star. When Helen saw him, she called out, "George." He looked up in total surprise, and from the look on his face, he was mentally searching and trying to recall from where he might remember this lovely American lady. After talking with Helen briefly, he kindly wrote a short note and autographed her program. This was a very exciting moment for Helen because she secretly adored George Peppard, enjoyed his movies and television programs. After all, he was so handsome with his gray hair, and he always played his movie roles so well.

The evening was young as the duo headed for Stringfellows, a private club. At the door, they met a fine young man named Antoine, originally from Holland. He was working in Luxemburg and looking for a night out with the ladies. Since it was a private club, where possibly some royalty might attend, he was not allowed to enter. Immediately, the girls stepped in and invited him to be their guest from the hotel. Antoine wanted to dance with them and escorted them all evening. They enjoyed the dancing to the disco music and noticed a very strange sensation called a "mirage." Once the smoke and lasers appeared on the dance floor, it seemed like their feet never touched the ground. This gave them a feeling of dancing on air. It was the most incredible feeling Helen and Margaret had ever experienced while dancing. They would welcome the opportunity to feel that magic again.

After an early breakfast the next day, the search was on to find Buckingham Palace. Margaret's cousin, Dennis, took them right past the other guards. They quickly followed Dennis and found the area where the horses were stabled. For the past twenty years, Dennis had taken care of the queen's magnificent horses, and Helen wanted to pet them. The horse-drawn carriages were always ready for ceremonial functions, for parliament, and for the queen's personal use. Dennis invited Margaret and Helen into his flat at the palace for a cup of tea and cakes in the muse. Before they left the castle, the girls were able to watch the changing of the guard, and the guards sure looked good standing in line at attention.

Later in the day, the girls were off to the Palace Theater, where they paid a hefty sum for tickets. Along the route to the theater, busy traffic on the narrow streets made crossing difficult. The walk was like finding one's way through a maze, as many of the old theaters were being refurbished with large scaffolds on the streets. It was unbelievable to see lines of people waiting for someone to give up their tickets, so they could see the play. They saw the well-known *Les Misérables*, which proved to be well worth the high price of admission. The musical's plot was good, and the singing was outstanding. You could almost feel the presence of God Almighty in the theater that day.

Helen and Margaret were soon on the go again, and Helen had her first fright of the day. Margaret was in her usual fast pace, with Helen readily following behind. For just a moment, she lost sight of Margaret when Margaret turned a corner. When Helen quickly turned the corner, she could see Margaret with her eyes bulging in her worry over losing her good friend. Oh, happy days, she wasn't really lost after all, and you can almost imagine how terrified she was, for fear of being all alone and lost in a foreign country.

Soon, the pair was happily riding a bright red, double-decker bus. As Helen sat on the upper deck, she felt like she was on top of the world, with a picturesque view of London's beautiful bridges on the scenic waterways and Big Ben. There always seemed to be crowds of people in a hurry rushing to and fro.

Helen made a discovery as the taxies sped around the circle, narrowly missing them as they walked past. It seemed strange to see a roundabout in the middle of the square. When she mentioned the oddity to the people standing around, they seemed to laugh at her remark. Possibly, her American accent must have seemed strange to the British residents.

They toured Oxford Circus, Covent Square, and Regent Square for some shopping and Piccadilly Circus and other downtown stores. Helen knew about money and quickly learned about pounds and pence. She soon became aware that the American dollar bought a lot less here than it did at home. The trip to London was an educational and expensive learning experience.

A short time later, it was time for their ride to join the Londoners on the underground subway to Leicester Square. The subway system was somewhat different than the ones Helen had ridden in New York City. The underground cars had also been used as shelters during the bombings in the Second World War. The subway was dimly lit and very deep in the ground. Unfortunately, the lift was out of order, and they were soon rapidly climbing up eight floors of steep, winding staircase. Helen and Margaret both seemed a little out of breath, and they noticed half of the busy Londoners panting as well. Helen asked herself why these people were racing in such a big hurry. The ascent was so tiring that they had to rest on one of the landings as they climbed. But when they looked back towards the seventh floor, there wasn't a soul following them. Helen and Margaret were able to prove their endurance climbing the stairwell.

THE AMAZING VENICE-SIMPLON ORIENT EXPRESS

The next morning, after a warm English breakfast, the ladies' chauffer drove them to the Venice-Simplon Orient Express at the famous Victoria Station. It was time to say ta ta to the world famous city of London.

The original Orient Express made its last regular run in 1977, after several decades of declining ridership. Various short-run trains continue to provide service over parts of the original orient Express.

At Folkstone, the girls promptly boarded the Sealink British ferries. Crossing the English Channel and passing over the Straits of Dover, the ferry ride was short. Helen thought of the song about the white cliffs of Dover, which was made famous during the Second World War. She excitedly pointed out the white cliffs of Dover to her friend Margaret, while the ferry passed over them. After an hour's ride, they arrived in Boulogne, France, and promptly boarded the Orient Express. They could hardly contain themselves as they were on their way for a delightful journey to Venice, Italy.

On the train, they later found themselves in the lounge, sitting very close to a handsome, young, dark-haired Italian piano player. Helen was soon able to exercise her vocal chords, singing her old-time favorite "Summer Time." Even though it was winter, the song more or less described the girls' sentiments, and it was nice to sit and enjoy some of their favorite songs, with Raefello at the piano.

During the journey on the Orient Express, the girls found it hard to sleep, as the train made several stops during the night, including Paris, Switzerland, Austria, and then on to Italy. Looking out the window on the train, they were able to watch the pretty white snow coming down quite heavily in Austria and the many high mountain Alps. As the train passed through Switzerland and Austria, it seemed a little strange to see the land change from freezing white snow to warmer brown land as they enjoyed their long ride throughout Italy. While they slept, the train traveled all night through Europe.

Interestingly, Helen and Margaret did not feel tired and, furthermore, were not at all hungry. Stephen from Scotland had just finished serving those delicious English cakes and tea.

ROMANTIC VENICE, ITALY
WITH MANY SIGHTS TO SEE

As evening arrived, the girls came to Santa Lucia station in Venice. Their guide picked them up and arranged for a water taxi ride to the Monaco-Grand Canal Hotel. They learned that cars were not allowed, and everything had to be done by boat. Dumbstruck, they watched in amazement as some furniture was being moved on a small boat.
Venice was a lovely city, with over 80,000 residents. The city wove its way through the picturesque canals, especially enchanting at night, when the girls could hear the ringing of the nearby church bells.

They visited the Basilica de Marco at Marco Square, watching groups of pigeons that seemed to be standing by just waiting. Visiting the many shops was a lot of fun. They'd heard that Venice was a romantic city and found this to be very true.

Tired upon arrival, the girls overslept the next morning and thought it would be nice to feel regal and have breakfast served in bed. Margaret woke up fearing she had a problem with her eye and wanted to get to a hospital to have it checked out. They found a nearby hospital, and Margaret was able to see a French physician. The hospital was clean with a capable staff, and after checking her out, the physician told Margaret she would be okay. They were both surprised to hear that there would not be a fee for the good service. This was amazing—only in Venice!

As they traveled, Helen and Margaret stopped to visit and pray at several of the older churches in the square.

Their next stop was inside the square at the Murano glass blowing factory, where they watched the glassblowers carefully make magnificent crystal and glass figurines.
Helen was overwhelmed as she watched the skilled artisans blow the glass, and she bought an exquisite mirrored tray and a blue glass coffee set with matching glasses to be shipped to America.

After a tiring afternoon in the damp, chilly air, the girls headed to dinner. They stopped at a small Italian café for some enjoyable Italian food. Later, it was time to head back to the hotel for some rest, warmth, and a quiet sleep. Upon arriving at their hotel, they noticed an American couple standing in front, noticeably upset. While they waited for a taxi, some thieves had grabbed their belongings. Helen and Margaret felt bad for the couple, and the episode made them more cautious during their trip in Venice.

The next morning at 8:00 a.m. sharp, they awoke to the loud ringing of the telephone. It only took them a half hour to wake up, open the automatic shutters, take a hot bath, and drag their tired bodies down to the restaurant. The Petit Dejeuner featured hot coffee, hot milk for their coffee, croissants, and little jars of jam.

The sun was shining, but it was a cool, damp morning as they set off on foot to the newly familiar Marco Square. They crossed several canals over some bridges and stopped to try on the beautiful clothes in the shops they passed. It was chilly, so they stopped to enjoy hot chocolate before heading back to their hotel.

At 3:00 p.m., they picked up their tour tickets. The tour guide was dressed like an army general and, furthermore, looked like one, in his loosely fitted brown coat. When he lifted his arms to describe a painting, Margaret noticed that his coat had a slit under one arm. He described a Titian painting at the Basilica de Frari, which was built in 1687.

They traveled farther down the street, leaving this strong religious influence to observe Gothic architectural designs. After crossing a few more of the many scenic bridges, all twelve of the tourist group got in the two large gondolas crossing the canal. You could almost laugh watching them, as they precariously put one foot on the step and one foot on the gondola. Six of the tourists were paddling on their way to the famous Rialto Bridge in Venice. They began to feel like they were in a movie scene as they were busy riding and rowing in a gondola in Venice. The time had come to say good-bye, "arrivederci" to their tall, Gestapo-looking guide, with the big nose. Helen would not leave without questioning him as to how often he tolerated these tours. He said he made his tours seven days a week for two hours a day. He kept a busy schedule with very little time to sew up the slit in his brown coat.

As they continued their tour of the city, the girls felt the chill in the air but found their way through the market, looking at sweaters, handbags, and mostly, jewelry. Since they were starving and needed a bit of warmth, they fell into a most welcome sidewalk café. They ordered a plate of lasagna. The spaghetti was delicious and was served with a jug of Chianti wine, which made Margaret and Helen feel warm inside. They ate heartily, thoroughly enjoying the lasagna dinner. The waiter half-willingly sang a few bars of an Italian song but soon disappeared because of his shyness. As Margaret would say, "Maybe he felt we didn't show enough respect." Paying the bill had become a nervous ritual because they were convinced that everybody was trying to cheat the American ladies out of their money.
At 9:00 a.m. the next morning, the waiter knocked at the door, bringing up an assortment of rolls, butter, and small jars of jam; a flank of chocolate; and a jug of tea. It was a nice day, and the sun was brightly shining without the interruption of a cloud.

The same birds that dominated Marco Square still produced a carpet of pigeons everywhere. Sitting at the hotel bar, Helen and Margaret looking through the clear glass windows into an edge of orchids nestled in dark green leaves. The Grand Canal was busy with graceful gondolas, and many tourists above the canal enjoyed their lunch in the warm sunshine.

An interesting point to note was that a cup of coffee cost five American dollars (five thousand Italian lire). It seemed like a lot of money to count. Shortly, the girls left Venice for their pleasant ride via a water taxi to the station.

Could Hardly Wait for a Visit to Rome:
Seemed so Exciting and Far from Home

After a pleasant train ride at 7:00 p.m., Rome appeared on the horizon. The girls had a good night's rest and were up bright and early the next morning, as they eagerly looked ahead to their tour of Rome. They were blessed with what one would call a good and wholesome breakfast. It consisted of an abundance of choices of fresh fruits, cereals, soft Italian cheeses, pears, and steaming hot coffee. Having enjoyed a hearty breakfast, Helen and Margaret were ready to explore the city, where they could visit the fabulous shops, avenues, and churches. Soon they discovered the Spanish Square and decided to take a horse-and-buggy ride, where they could sit back and discover the city. Refusing to meet the driver's price of 50,000 lira, Helen suggested they share the ride at half the cost. Soon they promoted two English tourists from the Isle of Wight in their pursuit.

They shared in the cost of the ride. The Italian driver became greedy and asked for 70,000 lira, and Helen went back to the bargaining table. They were soon enjoying their short tour around the Spanish Square at a cost of 60,000 lira. Stopping at the Square, they walked around a water fountain where local artists were selling their artwork. An historic church appeared before their eyes, and they walked inside to have a good look and pray. Several stops were made at some shops with the sound of the horse hoofs tapping on the cobbled streets. While riding through the square, the girls noticed that the horses appeared urgent to hurry home as they neared the return to fresh hay and water. They weaved their way through strange roads back to their hotel.

Once again, Helen and Margaret met with their tour guide, who connected them with a bus tour that would stop at various points of interest; including Piazza San Bernardo; Fontana dell' Acqua Felice (the Fountain of Moses); Piazza della Repubblica, with the Fountain of the Naiads; Via Nacionale; Piazza Venezia, with the Memorial to King Victor Emanuel II and the Tomb of the Unknown Soldier; Capitoline Hill (visit); a panoramic view of the Roman Forum and the Palatine Hill; the Synagogue Imperial Foro; the Colosseum; the Arch of Constantine; Circus Maximus; the Adventure Hill; St. Paul's Gate; Pyramid of Caius Cestius; Basilica St Paul; the

Domus Aurea; Tito's Bath; Church of St. Peter in Chains with the Statue of Moses by Michelangelo (visit).

At the Colosseum, their guide informed them, as it was contrary to past belief, that Nero was not present at the lion slaying of Christians at the arena. Nero, he explained, wasn't even born at the time. This was so contrary to the myth Helen and Margaret had been accustomed to hearing.

Standing in front of St. Peter's Church, the girls were enthralled to see the marble statue of Moses.

After a day of sightseeing, Margaret and Helen were tired and grateful to return to the comforts of the Hotel Ingleteria, as their bodies and feet were in need of recovery.

After a short rest, they asked some friendly Italians along the way for directions to the Tritorian Restaurant. They soon found the pizzeria, where they watched a young girl cooking and tossing the dough, giving a one-two turn. After dinner, they went in search of a disco for dancing. They were disappointed because Gilda, the disco they were looking for, was not open on Fridays.

It was time to move on to meet Mr. Wonderful, a man named Jay who was from Fort Worth, Texas. It appeared that Helen always seemed to meet men by the name of Jay. The girls enjoyed some drinks with their new friend, Jay, who insisted they try an Italian drink known as grappa. They later learned that grappa was an undiluted version of grapes in the purest sense of the word.

The lack of both sleep and the accustomed diet of American food were catching up with the girls, and they found themselves staggering. Unable to resist the elegant shop windows, in spite of their twisted ankles and sore feet, they somehow managed to begin trying on beautiful clothes, shoes, and jewelry. Helen bought some more clothes and was delighted with the beautiful red wool coat with attached hood she found, as it would keep her warm. She began to feel a little like Little Red Riding Hood as she walked carefully in the night through the damp, cold streets of Italy.

Back at the hotel Margaret and Helen once again flopped in their beds, trying to re-energize their tired bodies. They needed a short rest as they were planning to enjoy a nice evening out on the town. At the hotel they, left behind their thermal underwear in place of light stockings and shoes for their last evening in Rome.

In the Garden Room at the Ingleterria Hotel, their day ended with a delightful gourmet dinner. It wasn't very long before they found interesting company—a Frenchman who was staying at the hotel between flights and an elderly English couple. They enjoyed the evening, sharing several bottles of wine and champagne.

Margaret became a bit nervous when she noticed a gentleman in a corner of the room just sitting there watching them very carefully. After a while, she questioned him and took his picture for future reference. It turned out he was a bodyguard for the French gentleman.

Frankfurt, Germany, and Heading Home

The hotel wake-up call rang sharply at 4:00 a.m. Shortly, thereafter, a tired alarm followed, and the mad dash began. Sadly, the journey was nearing an end, and it was time to pack up and leave the grand hotel. After many purchases, the girls wondered how they were going to get all of their belongings stuffed in their bags. They even placed some things on top of their luggage. The limo arrived promptly, and they bid Rome farewell as they traveled through the dimly lit, deserted streets. They arrived at the airport with ample time for the early 7:00 a.m. departure to Frankfurt, Germany.

The short flight to Frankfurt was comfortable, but upon disembarking the plane, the girls soon felt the fear of German aggression descending upon them. With their heavy luggage secured on wheels, they proceeded with effort to the Delta check-in counter. When they attempted to go through a gap in the line, a strange-looking man almost jumped over their wheels, as he was so fearful the ladies were going to take his place. When the girls asked for directions, a German porter barely raised his arm in what they imagined to be a Gestapo gesture, waving them to the left. As they were a very bright species, they seemed to realize what the direction meant. They promptly took off, as the crow flies, in that direction. Once in line, they thought they knew how it felt to be in a spy movie. They were interrogated and questioned over and over; Margaret to begin to worry that she might possibly have something bad in her bags. After reading through Margaret's passport, the female German interrogator asked her, "While you were in Tunisia, did you associate with any natives?"

Margaret deftly replied, her eyes wide open to convey honesty, "I was there with my husband," lest the interrogator thought Margaret had had an affair with one of the natives or had possibly sold someone illegal weapons. You could see the fear in Margaret's face as she slowly looked around for support from anything she could have contact with. All she could see was her friend Helen, who had a huge grin on her face, not realizing the seriousness of the situation. So Margaret bravely continued, "I don't remember, as it was three or four years ago."

"Were you with a group?" the German interrogator questioned.

Margaret replied, "I don't think so."

The interrogator seemed satisfied with Margaret's defense and sternly asked her to move on.

It was then Helen's turn to be questioned. "Do you have any weapons in your bag?" the woman asked. (I am just kidding.)

Helen replied, "I don't think so, but I have a camera."

Then the interrogator asked if the women had anything electrical. Of course, they didn't, except that Margaret had her hair dryer. Their anguish was obvious, as they were fearful for any further delay, which could possibly become another problem. They hoped that it would not be necessary to take their luggage off the plane for a search for some hidden bombs.

They had the strange feeling that they were not in control at the Frankfurt Airport. When they were given the stamp of approval, they were very happy to be on their way home to America.

Their plane arrived in Orlando after a ten-hour, tiring, and uneventful trip. Going through customs, the girls declared the required purchases, including Helen's hooded red coat. Their trip to London, Venice, Rome, and the Orient Express was coming to an end. It had been exciting and eventful and would remain a happy memory for a lifetime to come.

Back Home at Spruce Creek, Daytona Beach, Florida

Another incident occurred while Jay Jay was fishing on a small lake at Spruce Creek with his school friends. The group was fishing directly behind the home that a famous film star was renting while making a movie nearby. He complained to security and the association manager, requesting that the young men leave because he needed privacy at his home. Jay Jay informed security that he had no intention of leaving the lake where he was quietly fishing. He said his parents had been owners of several properties since the beginning of the development. He knew the lakes were part of the community. Therefore, Jay Jay and his friends continued to fish.

A short time later, another very famous movie star and long time owner of his home at Spruce Creek, who was playing golf nearby, stopped to chat with the young men in his usual friendly manner. "Are the fish biting?" he asked.

After Jay Jay showed the star a large bass, he mentioned the problem of the man's friend. He wanted the man to tell the visiting star that he put his pants on the same way and had no desire to peek in anybody's windows. He also mentioned his mom, Helen, who the star knew from their business and real estate dealings.

Since this particular star lived in the neighborhood, he would stop by the office on occasion to visit and chat with Helen. One afternoon, she invited him to come to her home to look at some equipment after he'd stopped at her office. Linda and her friend, Michelle, were sitting at the kitchen table, and introductions were soon made. He looked over the exercise equipment and surveyed the room, taking in the many interesting antiques. While upstairs, his eyes focused on a large picture of himself when he was much younger on Linda's bedroom door. Helen quickly reached for her pen, and he autographed his picture and wrote a little note to Linda for a keepsake. After the house tour was over, he came down and set his coffee cup in the kitchen sink, close to where the girls were still sitting. He seemed to be having some difficulty finding the door, as he left through a side door. The house had a turret and was similar to a small castle; navigating through it would be somewhat confusing on one's first visit. Anyway, Helen reached in the sink and handed him his cup, though it would have made a nice souvenir to keep. Upon his request, she would also perform notary services at his home. She would also help out and sell him some properties that were difficult to obtain at Spruce Creek.

One year, close to Christmastime, Helen was at the Daytona Airport watching their large jet being loaded as they were getting ready for takeoff. As she walked through the gate, she heard a voice calling her name. Looking back, she saw her movie star friend sitting in the car with his wife and baby, and Helen was introduced to them.

A short time later, their plane was ready for takeoff and Helen waved them off. It reminded Helen of the many times that she would wave to him before takeoff from her home on the taxiway at Spruce Creek. He was a very special person who always appeared to be warm and friendly.

One day, Helen rented a home at Spruce Creek to a famous country western singer. Before long, the singer dropped by her office, requesting a private visit to see her well-known movie star friend. It seems they knew each other from way back when, and he thought it would be fun to reconnect. They made the trip in his white limo, and Helen enjoyed a fun-filled visit with some great guys, as they talked about the old times and some of the famous people they both knew in the movie industry. The tour was enjoyable, and they refused the kind offer for refreshments.

Sadly, their wonderful movie star needed more room for his airplanes and moved to another place in Florida. All the folks would miss him, and Helen hoped to see him on the screen in the movies.

Helen was having difficulty with her new neighbor as they shared a taxiway easement. The easement was granted to her and her neighbor in order to allow for more room for the airplanes to come in and out of the hangars. Helen allowed her nice doctor friend to use the space to hangar his plane. Then the nasty neighbor decided to plant some trees in the path of the easement and did not allow Helen's doctor friend to use her taxiway. The taxiway access was blocked, no longer allowing the plane to get out to the runway. When the good doctor spoke to the nasty neighbor, he was told to get his plane out or he might find some sugar in his engine. A fight ensued as the neighbor struck the doctor. It seemed safer to move his plane than to continue fighting with the nasty neighbor, and Helen could find another use for the airplane hangar.

The problem was soon solved, as she used the space for a valuable car collection. Many of the drivers who raced at the Daytona track stayed at the Spruce Creek Fly-In Airport, enabling them to fly and park their jets close to home. A very famous race car driver rented the house next door to Helen for the racing season. He had difficulty getting his airplane onto the taxiway at the back of his rented home and agreed to help Helen take care of her problem with the easement and the nasty man. The problem ended when he went into the hangar, got out a chainsaw, and quickly cut the troublesome trees down. This made Helen very happy.

While Jay Jay was in high school, Helen bought him a nice Volvo so he could get around safely with good transportation. He had the opportunity to work on a part-time basis on expensive, custom-built homes. From the very beginning, Jay Jay was a good worker and very creative. He learned a lot about building homes, which seemed to be becoming a family tradition.

One day after work, Helen came home and went into the hangar, and to her amazement, she discovered Jay Jay and some of his close friends skateboarding at high speeds up and down the newly built ramp in the hangar. It was not only dangerous, but Helen feared that if someone fell and got hurt, she'd be facing a lawsuit. She asked him to remove the intricately designed ramp. Soon, a golf-pro friend of Jay Jay's stopped in the hangar to check out the special skateboard ramp, as skateboarding was a new phase around the country at the time. He liked what he saw and bought the ramp from Jay Jay. A short time later, his friend started up a skateboard park in the Daytona area for the youngsters.

As soon as high school was over, Jay Jay made his plans. His mind was made up—he would enlist in the army, anticipating a tour of duty in Hawaii for three years. He was determined that he could pay for his college education on his own, using the GI Bill. Helen feared he might be more interested in surfing the giant waves in Hawaii than in his future schooling.

While waiting for his orders from the army, Jay Jay spent a lot of his free time chasing the pretty young ladies around town. One evening, he had been following some young men as they left a local club. An argument ensued over the girls, which caused an accident with minor damage to the young man's car. Jay Jay conveniently forgot to mention the accident. Helen was quite surprised when a young policeman was at her front door to talk about the incident and give her a phone number to call.

Helen, Linda, and Jay Jay met with the stranger so they could discuss the matter further. It was purely a coincidence that the week before Helen had met the young man's nephew, whose car Jay Jay had damaged. She had been trying to sell the man some vacant land at Spruce View. The foreign stranger appeared to be nice and friendly when they met with him at his condo. Helen agreed to take care of the damages, and all ended well. They all soon became acquainted, as Helen helped him with advice on his real estate properties. Their new acquaintance turned out to be a very powerful man in the world of foreign intrigue.

Time passed quickly, and the youngsters had become grown-ups. Linda went off to continue her studies at Florida State University, with hopes of working in the television industry.

While Linda was away at college studying communications and broadcasting, she took a trip to Boston to visit some friends from an international soccer team. Before long, she wanted to visit New York City to scout around the TV stations. To help Linda get started, Helen ignored any danger surrounding their friend of intrigue and called upon him to inquire whether he might have any connections that would help Linda in her endeavor. He promptly made some hasty arrangements for his sister to meet Linda in New York City and take her around to the local TV stations. Fate stepped in; That morning, New York City had a bad snowstorm, and Linda missed her life's calling in broadcasting. Sadly, she was unable to meet with man of intrigue's sister, who had been patiently awaiting her arrival. Isn't it amazing how one makes different choices due to circumstances, and unexplained events can change one's course along life's road.

Linda finished her required courses at Florida State University and the

University of Central Florida. Now she is a teacher—one of those teachers who are truly dedicated to their work—in the Orlando area.

Off to Las Vegas, a Fun Place to Go: Take the Time and Enjoy the Show

In April 1991, Helen and Margaret were on their way to the Orlando Airport, with a short stop at the Delta Crown Room They were in need of some cool refreshments to take off the edge of flying, as they were waiting to board a plane bound for Las Vegas.

Upon their arrival, the girls picked up a new red Cadillac Seville at the Alamo Rent A Car. They stayed on the seventieth floor at the Flamingo Hilton. Their first stop was as Circus Circus, where they kept busy with a lot of fun games. There were many exciting things to see, including an inside tram with a lot of carnival-style amusements. In the evening, the girls enjoyed a lobster and steak dinner at the Star Dust Inn, for a surprisingly low price of three dollars and ninety cents.

At the Desert Inn, the feature attraction was "Champions on Ice," with a cast of gold-medal winners. Margaret and Helen thoroughly enjoyed the great performance from their front-row seats, even as some of the ice was hitting them. Amazingly, twenty years ago, Margaret had been an ice-skater on this same stage, and the show must have been a nice reminder of days gone by. When the show was over, Margaret sent brave Helen backstage to personally meet all the skaters. She bravely asked the skaters if they were in the show, and she told them she had enjoyed the ice-skating as they all kindly signed her program.

After waiting out back, Margaret finally found the courage to go backstage and introduce Helen to the stage manager. He remembered Margaret and told them some interesting stories about some of the old movie stars. Over the years, many famous stars had performed at the Desert Inn. It would always be a special night to remember.

Helen and Margaret's next day began with a visit to the famed Caesar's Palace. They had lots of fun winning and losing at the slot machines. Later, they stopped in at the Omni Theatre and saw the movie *Blue Planet*, which was informative as to the world's awakening about the earth's pollution.

In the evening, they feasted at the Excalibur Hotel while watching a great show. The normal practice was for everyone to eat the delicious food with their hands, at the same time banging on the tables and stomping on the floors throughout the performance. It seemed somewhat unusual to act in this manner, but everyone was doing it.

A short time later, they were off to the Mirage Hotel, where they watched a combination of many incredible diversions, including a volcano that erupted every few minutes and white tigers walking around in caves, with only water and glass to keep them from attacking the people. The tigers were simply beautiful. They were also tame, and you almost wanted to reach out and touch them, as if making nice to little teddy bears. Later on, one of the tigers would get spooked and attack one of the trainers, Roy, injuring him very seriously. Today, he's lucky to be alive, and sadly, after so many years, they closed the show. The show was breathtaking and dangerous, and it drew large crowds for many years.

Naturally, the evening was topped off with wonderful music and dancing. Margaret and Helen found dance partners rather quickly. One of Helen's new dance partners danced with her while his bodyguards stood on guard. They enjoyed the beat, dancing into the night.

After a hurried breakfast the next morning, the girls drove to the northwestern section of the city, where they viewed the snowcapped Frenchman's Mountain and Mt. Charleston. For lunch, they went to Pablo's Restaurant at the Santa Fe Hotel. Slot machines could be heard and seen everywhere. The restaurant included an ice-skating rink, a bowling alley, and a bingo hall. There was also music for dancing at the hotel in one of the buildings. It would be easy to stay for a long time and have a lot of fun. There was a lot to do to occupy their time and plenty of excitement. They drove by an area called Spanish Trails, where lots sold for a million dollars each; the prices seemed unreal for this desert property in this day in time.

In the comedy music club at the Bally's Hotel they watched "Catch a

Rising Star." Again, Margaret managed to get front-row seats. Helen and Margaret enjoyed the show, finding it to be very funny and entertaining.

In the evening, the girls made it to the Tropicana, where they saw an incredible show, *Folies Bergère*. Luckily, they were, once again, able to get front-row seats.

After they enjoyed dinner at the Java Room, Helen and Margaret immediately made a run for the slots. Las Vegas was a most amazing, fun-filled town, created in the barren desert of Nevada. A city that never sleeps, it was an exciting place, with various types of amusements and more nightlife than time would allow. At 4:00 a.m., you might find Margaret upstairs sleeping, but Helen found it difficult to leave the slots and would keep busy playing them. When she was winning, she would sometimes take over three machines at one time.

At the airport, the girls waited to board their plane; time was running short before takeoff. Helen continued to play the game of chance, trying to win all the Las Vegas money. But this too would come to an end, and it was time to leave the fun and slot machines. Las Vegas was a great place to escape, and Helen could hardly wait to return!

He's in the Army Now, and Off to Hawaii He Goes To An Island Where the Lava Sometimes Flows

Jay Jay went off to the army and was stationed in Hawaii for three years. This gave him an opportunity to enjoy his surfing, and said it didn't quite work out that way. Shortly before going into the service, Jay Jay met Monica. They were very young and in love. Since they did not want to separate, Monica joined him in Hawaii. While Jay Jay was on tour, Monica gave birth to their son, John Christopher (J. C.), named after his granddad, Jay, on November 19, 1992. Grandpa Jay must be watching from above, proud of his namesake.

One day, while Jay was alive, he'd asked Helen if she thought people came back to earth in their children after they'd died. It was truly amazing that their children looked and acted like them. Life was a mystery, and they would just have to see.

After they returned to the states from Hawaii, Jay Jay and Monica were having marital difficulties and filed for a divorce. They made the best of the situation, arranging for joint-custody, which allowed them to share in John's upbringing and care.

Jay Jay soon tired of the big city life in Daytona and bought a run-down trailer home that was in foreclosure on five acres in the country. He would have room to spread out and a place for his grown-up toys. Through hard work and foresight, he rebuilt the trailer home, starting with the foundation. This place in the country was ideal, as Jay Jay had always loved the outdoors. Like his father, Jay Jay knew how to get things done, and sometimes to perfection, and he started Spruce Creek Tree Service.

TIME FOR THE MEXICAN CONNECTION: HEADING IN THE RIGHT DIRECTION

In November 1995, after a long time in planning, Helen decided it was a good time to travel to Mexico. Upon arrival at the Port Manatee Dock in Tampa, Helen, Anna and John, along with their friend, Chantal, boarded the *Regal Princess* of *Princes Cruises*.

Early in the afternoon, the group enjoyed dance lessons, but in the background they heard the bells of the busy slot machines ringing, calling them to come play in the casino. Helen first tried the quarter machines, even though she was losing money. She whispered to the machines to wait for her as she would soon be back.

In the early evening, it was time for dinner at late seating, where they enjoyed good company and delicious food. They ended the evening with dancing to beautiful music in the Mermaid Lounge and the Grand Lounge. Their day had started at 5:00 a.m., and they were tired when they finally brought the evening to a close.

One of the highlights of another day was the beautiful music, dancing, and costumes for the masquerade at the Grand Lounge. They all participated in line dancing, ballroom dancing, and square dancing. The group on the ship kept on grooving while the beat went on. After the show and lots of dancing, they were off to bed, dreaming about tomorrow and their upcoming adventure in the Mayan ruins in Mexico.

They barely heard the ringing of the telephone at 4:30 a.m. They had to hurry, get breakfast, and wait for the tender to take them on to Playa del Carmen. Chantal, Anna, and Helen were in the dining room having a hearty breakfast and were surprised to run into Anna's husband, John. They expected him to be sawing logs somewhere in dreamland, but he wanted to wish them well because he knew he would miss them. The tender dropped the women off on the mainland of Mexico near the Playa del Carmen. Their cruise ship sailed on, and they later met it at Cozumel. Their informative and well-educated guide, Patrice (of Mayan descent), was waiting for them with a bus for the trip to the Mayan ruins at Tulum.

The Mayan Ruins in the Yucatan at Tulum

At last, they were finally off to see the ancient ruins in the Yucatan Peninsula, the ancient wall of Tulum and Xel-Ha Lagoon. As they traveled along the bumpy coastal road, the women noticed a lot of devastation caused earlier by Hurricane Roxanne. They saw a lot of activity as people worked to rebuild buildings and huts. Amazingly, the Mayans were able to use the palm fronds from the date palms and a little cement. This would keep their roofs from leaking and the rain could not seep through. It was a warm and sunny day, and the group was excited. After a wait of over three decades, they could see the Mayan ruins.

The guide talked about the culture and history of the Mayans and about a strange mark that would appear on all Mayans. As the Mayans grew older, the birthmark would amazingly seem to lighten into the color of their skin. The buildings were very interesting with their own story to tell. While learning the characteristics of the Mayans of long, long ago, the group walked along the ruins in wonder.

After a long walk in the very hot sun, seeing the sights and taking pictures, followed by a walk along the beach, the group was ready to get back to their bus. Helen called out to Chantal to hurry and leave with the group. They had to keep moving along, or they would be left behind. Chantal said she was busy loading her camera, and then she disappeared. Soon, Anna and Helen noticed the quiet all around them and started looking for Chantal.

With none of the group in sight, they called for Chantal. Terror gripped the sisters. They couldn't find Chantal, as she seemed to be nowhere in sight. They feared that the worst had befallen their friend. Why didn't she answer? Where was she? The stillness brought more fear. They were in a foreign country and hated to go without Chantal, but they didn't want to miss their waiting bus. As the golf cart with the group was leaving the ruins, Anna and Helen shouted for the group not to leave them behind as they ran the distance for the tram. Out of breath, they caught the tram and hopped aboard for their ride back to the waiting tour bus.

When the bus driver counted heads, he noticed Chantal was missing and held up the bus for a half hour, hoping she would arrive. Their very worried tour guide, Patrice, left one of his aides to wait for a sign of Chantal. Sadly, the bus headed on to the scheduled stop—a beautiful private lagoon called Xel-Ha Park, without their friend.

In the meantime, Chantal had gotten busy having a Spanish conversation with some other tourists at the ruins. She was enjoying herself and forgot all about the waiting bus. When she faced the reality that her friends had left her, she was not afraid, as she spotted Freddie, the guide's assistant, waiting for her. She called him her cute Mexican doll. Chantal and the assistant took a taxi to the park, where she soon met up with the group.

Xel-Ha was an incredibly beautiful park, which was being rebuilt with new plantings and buildings. Hurricane Roxanne had left in its wake a lot of devastation throughout the park and beach area. The warm, sandy beaches and blue waters with many tropical fishes brought the natural beauty in the park from imagination to reality. Divers came from many parts of the world to enjoy nature's kaleidoscope of colorful fish, scenic sights, and swaying tropical palm trees. They were told they could swim for a short time but were not allowed to use suntan lotion or chemicals. They wanted the waters to remain clean and in their natural state.

The reunited traveling friends bought some gifts while they visited a few gift shops. Once again, Helen lost her footing when she was stepping off the step at the gift shop leaving her badly bruised. She was unable to get up because of the pain, and help was soon on the way. Two male attendants carried her to the medical station, and medical attention was promptly administered. Sadly, the fall meant an end to Helen's dancing for the rest of the cruise. While on the ride back to the cruise ship, Helen and Chantal readily signed releases assuring the tour company that they wouldn't file any lawsuits in Mexico.

After they returned to the *Regal Princess*, they enjoyed a wonderful dinner. As tired as they were, they managed to play the slot machines at the Casino late into the night.

Except for a few minor incidents and falls, the trip was informative and pleasant. The food, company, and the service turned out to be just wonderful, and they would do it again, as the beat goes on. Viva la Mexico.

Stories Would Be Told as they Continued to Unfold

Helen enjoyed living in her little castle at #2 Lazy Eight Drive in Daytona for a period of ten years. After buying the lot next door, it was time to move on. The design for her new home, to be built at #4 Lazy Eight Drive, was a contemporary style. Planning and designing her little masterpiece was a lot of fun. A tropical lily pond stocked with colorful Koi fish was the highlight of the design.

After Linda left the university in Tallahassee, she searched for work in Orlando and was hired as a manager for a racetrack store. One day, a handsome man named Peter took an interest in a beautiful young lady at the store. It was our Miss Linda. She knew from the beginning that Pete was the man after her heart, and they seriously started dating.

After working in the real world for one year, she decided to go back to school. She earned her master's degree at the University of Central Florida and was able to get a good job in teaching.
Her first interview landed her a position with the Little River Elementary School. She was going to be a third-grade teacher and make a big difference in the education of her young students. It all seemed so natural, and Linda knew that she had found her calling in teaching. Many times after class, the students, as well as the parents, would stay and meet with Linda. They would stop in to talk with their favorite teacher, and it seemed that the

young minds of tomorrow needed her more than broadcasting did. Linda's smiling face was there for the little ones who looked up to her.

The Bahamas Mystery Cruise
on the *S.S. Atlantic*

In February 1996, Anna, John, Chantal, and Helen boarded a Big Red Boat cruise ship at Cape Canaveral. Without much delay, the ship set sail for Nassau. There was a feeling of excitement upon boarding, as the passengers were aware that a mystery was about to unfold in the "Cruise to Die For" series. It was obvious that the cruise company had stepped up security to ensure the safety of one of the world's most fabulous jewels, known as the Star of India Sapphire.

When the passengers arrived in their cabin on the Continental deck, they found champagne on ice awaiting their onboard toast. There was lots of room to move about, and they enjoyed the magnificent sunset from the port window each day. While waiting to leave port, they went up on the pool deck to enjoy their "Welcome Aboard" buffet.

After the usual lifeboat drill and taking care of the luggage, the group promptly headed off to the gambling casino. Helen followed John to the dollar machines. Lady Luck was with Helen, as she quickly won one hundred fifty dollars on the dollar slots. While in Nassau, Helen would use her winnings to buy a pair of Annabell designer sunglasses.

In the evening, their dinner was served with the delicious taste of Italian cuisine. They listened to soft music while dining on their sumptuous meal in the domed Galaxy Dining Room. At 10:00 p.m., the group headed for Club Universe to meet Lady Bosnatch, who was holding a reception to show off her famous Star of India diamond. They were served champagne as they waited for the mystery to begin.

At times, they were so busy gambling at the casinos that they missed the Swinging Singles Champagne Party, Late Night Pizza, Cantina Blast Party, Voyages of Discovery at the Mercury Theater, live calypso reggae music, and the Midnight Mexican buffet. After the first night on board, the group was overfed, tired, and ready for a good night's rest.

They awoke to clear skies for their arrival at historic Nassau in the Bahamas. After enjoying a nutritious breakfast, they were soon ready to disembark at Prince George's Wharf along Bay Street. The passengers went their different ways, some visiting Salt Cay or Coral Island, others riding the Sunshine Glass-Bottom boats and still others taking the Nassau City tours.

On shore, the ladies enjoyed a shopping tour and had a superb lunch aboard ship.

They later hired a driver to take them to—where else?—the Atlantic Hotel on Paradise Island, as the casinos were again calling from across the island. It was a lot of fun to play the game of chance on the many different slot machines. Helen quickly lost her quarters. But on the way out she played the dollar machines with twenty dollars. After only one pull on the handle, she won one hundred dollars. Helen promptly left with her winnings in hand and happily headed back to the big red boat.

After formal pictures were taken, the group was off to the champagne reception at Club Universe with the captain and senior officers of the *StarShip Atlantic*. They enjoyed complimentary champagne and fine dancing with the Enterprise group. In the early evening, the ship sailed for Port Lucaya to the beat of the calypso music with its island vibes. The dinner theme for the evening was the Caribbean Island, and the cuisine was delicious.

As the plot thickened, they needed to stay on course and get back to the murder mystery. Later, it turned out that that Joanna Darling was really the missing niece of Lady Bosnatch and involved with the diamond mystery.

The midnight buffet in the Galaxy Dining Room was truly magnificent, with an outstanding array of food. The buffet was served with the Statue of Liberty molded in ice castles in the food.

Early at sunrise the next morning, they got ready for the next port of call, Port Lucaya. After a short ride aboard the tender to shore, they walked around the square looking in at some of the fine shops and then went on to the straw market. Hearing the young islanders beating their drums to the island music was pleasant.

On their last evening, the mystery was solved, and the lucky couple from Orlando who had solved the mystery won a cruise.

Arriving at Cape Canaveral after a healthy breakfast, Helen and crew quickly went through customs and were off to their waiting car for the ride home. During the ride, they met a darling couple, Mai and Steve, and learned how the couple had met in Viet Nam during the war. At age sixteen, Mai worked in the laundry room at the navy base where Steve was stationed. As promised, he sent for Mai three years later, marrying her in 1973 in California.

The group enjoyed the fun times of their trip, and it was good to be on land once again.

It's Magical: Come Along to the Mediterranean

With the sun shining brightly on the lovely morning of May 7, 1997, Anna, John, and Helen happily set out for their anticipated all-night direct flight to Turkey on Turkish Airways from busy Kennedy Airport in New York. They knew that, upon arrival in Turkey, they would enter a world with a different culture than theirs.

At 12:45 a.m. the next morning, they watched the sun come up as they were gazing out the window. They hadn't even been to sleep and could see that it was already daylight. It was unusual that they could not look ahead, as their eyes were blinded as a result of the angle of the sun. They kept busy on the airplane, playing cards, reading, and walking up and down the aisles.

Istanbul, Turkey: Crossroads of the World

Their arrival in Istanbul was a very pleasant surprise. This was the only city in the entire world built on two continents, with a link between the East and the West, the past and the present. Istanbul guards the precious relics of the three empires of which she has been the capital. It is an unforgettable city of intrigue, with a mystic charm, and Helen, Anna, and John found the people to be very friendly. As their eager eyes began to look around, they saw minarets and domes in an unchanging skyline, with an abundant variety of museums, palaces, ancient churches, mosques, and bazaars. Along the ancient cobbled streets, there was a continual movement of the crowds, alive with the sounds of busy street vendors near the ports.

Walking seemed to be the best way of getting around the narrow streets in such a busy city. They did not have to change their money, as the U.S. government had been very friendly with Istanbul, thereby making the U.S. dollar highly regarded in this country. The group noticed the dress code was different—the people wore an older style of clothing and were not dressed in shorts. In our modern times, the Turkish people were beginning to see a change, as the younger people dressed more casually. The rate of inflation was very high, and it seemed the people didn't have a lot of money to spend. Many older buildings crowded into every nook and cranny. The streets were kept clean, and the garbage was routinely picked up. Helen found some time to buy some lovely gold Byzantine jewelry at the hotel at special prices. She learned that there would not be a customs charge, as the United States had a trade agreement with Turkey, and this proved to be true when she declared the jewelry upon arrival at customs in New York.

After arriving and settling in at their first-class room at the Conrad Hotel, Helen, Anna, and John met some other travelers who had arrived from around the world to join them in their exciting cruise. As the group was getting hungry, they decided to go out to eat and take in some of the picturesque city sights on the way to dinner. After several inquiries, they were given directions in English and were soon on their way to eat.

To their dismay, as they walked along the crowded streets searching for a fancy restaurant with a good view of the Marmer River, it didn't take more than a short five minutes before they were lost in the hustle and bustle amidst the busy people. They all seemed to be racing by and climbing up the hills on the cobblestone streets. After traveling one block in their search for a good Turkish meal, they seemed to be lost again, and stopped to ask a man who didn't speak English for some directions. His attempts were futile, as he tried to give directions with raised hands, motioning the group down the street, his Turkish falling on uncomprehending ears. Since that didn't work, the group approached another Turkish gentleman, and he sent them in the right direction, with the suggestion that they call a taxi. Their taxi drove them around the corner, charged one U.S. dollar, and dropped them off at an elegant Turkish restaurant. How difficult was that?

After their arrival at the nice Turkish restaurant, the group was offered a choice of eating a meat meal downstairs or a meal of fish upstairs, and they chose to dine downstairs. The handsome, dark-haired owner of the restaurant was dressed in an expensive silk suit and was ready to serve them personally. He prepared his specialty meal with a variety of meats, chicken, lamb, and meatballs. The owner, as well as the waiters, stood nearby, continuously talking and filling their glasses with water. Not only was the company very enjoyable, the Turkish meal was also truly delicious, though Helen would say it was a little bit spicy. To Helen's surprise, as they left the restaurant, with all the waiters standing at the door watching, the handsome owner shook their hands and thanked them for coming to his restaurant. Everyone watched as all the waiters were standing nearby clapping and cheering, and they quickly rushed out the door.

Feeling happy and content after their very fine dinner, the travelers walked along the pier and sat down to watch the active ferryboats carrying some very friendly Turkish people across the still, blue waters. They felt like they were on parade, as they noticed that some of the people sitting on the benches were also watching them. With their fair skin and light-colored hair, they looked like strangers. When their pleasant street adventure was over, they hailed a cab to take them back around the block to their luxurious Conrad Hotel. After meeting and greeting some of their new friends who would be joining them at the hotel for the cruise, they visited the coffee shop for a quick pick-me-up, enjoying the strong taste of Turkish coffee and several delicious cakes.

After settling down in their room, Anna, John, and Helen played several games of cards. After Anna won all three games, they were a bit weary, and it was time to say good night.

At 4:45 a.m., they were awakened to a very loud siren—the usual call to prayer—, which lasted about fifteen minutes. It was so loud you can be sure it could wake up anybody and everybody. Of course, they went right back to sleep for some more rest. It seemed to Helen they might not need to sell a lot of alarm clocks in Turkey.

It was the custom to have time for prayer several times during the day, as well.

Their continental breakfast at the hotel was delightful and included delicious Turkish pastries. Again, they had strong, dark coffee and enjoyed nectar and juices. Pat, Bob, and Marty from San Francisco met them after breakfast. They soon became good friends and joined the trio on the Marco Polo adventure.

The fast ride through the narrow streets was a bit frightening. There were some tense moments, as the streets were so narrow that it was difficult for two cars to pass through at the same time. From the windows on the bus, the passengers watched people riding on scooters and others running or walking rapidly between the buses and even between the cars. After a terrifying bus ride, they arrived safely at the cruise line's entry gate. Two armed guards met the group and, after checking their passports, allowed them to board the *Marco Polo*. Their ship was an older ship, once owned by the Russian people and used as an icebreaker.

After their arrival, the trio had some good food on deck and returned to their cabins to put away their gear in their very crowded quarters with three bunk beds. As soon as they were out to sea, it was time to go to the casino and play the slot machines, though they had no luck. Early in the evening, they took the first seating in the nicely decorated Seven Seas restaurant. Thus began a journey into the greatest-tasting cuisine ever.

Kusadasi Rests on the Aegean Coast in Turkey With Interesting Sights Waiting for All to See

Kusadasi is built on the shores of a glittering bay around a tiny islet (Bird Island), which is covered with flowers and is one of the major gates of tourism in Turkey. It is a seaside resort town, starting point for excursions to the ancient cities of Ephesus, Priene, Miletus, and Didyma. Just off shore to the west of the town is the small island of Guvercin (Pigeon Island), which can be reached by a pedestrian causeway, where a fourteenth-century Turkish fortress now houses a café in a beautiful garden setting. A group of shops make up the town center, with many street peddlers selling their wares on the streets in front of the shops and on the waterfront. It would appear that the merchants were always ready to sell anything and everything. Anna and Helen stopped to buy some perfumes and socks for the family. They heard that the leather ware and Turkish rugs were being sold at very reasonable prices.

They were checking out the shops and soon met a nice shopkeeper, who immediately walked them over to his carpet warehouse. Throwing caution to the wind and without fear of any danger, the sisters innocently followed the shopkeeper behind some storage buildings. The room was dark, and he turned on lights along the way. Soon, they were busy climbing upstairs to a back room looking at carpets and jewelry. Admittedly, they were a little apprehensive, but they followed him anyway. He proceeded to display carpets, gold jewelry, and other items, explaining that it took one woman six months to weave a tiny silk carpet and quoted a price of three hundred dollars. The shopkeeper placed many beautiful silk carpets before them in an attempt to entice them to spend U.S. dollars. Being hospitable, he offered Anna and Helen a drink of apple tea, and he proved to be a fine gentleman, showing the sisters the masterful art of salesmanship. After leaving their new friend, they quickly found their way back downstairs to the front of the building.

The ladies soon approached another jewelry store. By this time, they were very thirsty and accepted some mineral water in a capped bottle. Of course, they were unable to make it out of the store without buying some lovely jewelry. It was very difficult to make their way back to the *Marco Polo* because there were so many vendors blocking their path. Somehow, they dodged the vendors and, luckily, made it back to the ship unharmed.

Back on the ship, Helen visited the gift shop and bought a useful safari hat to protect her from the blazing, hot sun and, hopefully, help her continue to look much younger than she was.

After a restful and enjoyable afternoon aboard ship, the trio once again headed to the Seven Seas restaurant, where they enjoyed a delicious prime rib dinner. Helen found a new friend, Nancy, who was a nurse on vacation from New Jersey. After dinner, the new friends promptly headed up to the pool deck for more dessert and to enjoy dreamy music with the Tower Orchestra. Later in the evening, they watched a Turkish group from the city perform a folklore show at the Paddock. It wasn't very long before they found the casino to try their good fortune. Helen won a little money, but at 1:00 a.m. she was told the casino was closing and it was time to leave.

Looking for Warmth and Peace
At the Island of Delos in Greece

The following morning, the ship docked at the island of Delos, which is an important archeological site in Greece. For almost one thousand years, Delos was known as the religious and political center of the Aegean and, every four years, was host to the Delian games, the region's greatest festival. The sanctuary flourished in the sixth and seventh centuries BC under the control of Naxos and was the main source of statues and other works of art. There was a purification of the island in 426 BC, when it became a rule that neither birth nor death was allowed on Sacred Delos. Pregnant women and those near death were transported to Rheneia for confinement or death. Later, Delos became an important commercial and political center for the Greek states. The island's festivals brought many of the people together, and it was well placed on trade routes. In 146 BC, the Romans gave Delos to the people of Athens, and the island became the busiest trading center in the Eastern Mediterranean. Many of the houses from that period of great wealth had survived. Delos is now a national park in Greece, and the island continues to remain one of the most important antiquities surviving from the ancient world.

Helen and Nancy toured Delos, walking among the ancient ruins and enjoying the picturesque landscape and the crystal clear, blue sea, with the scenic mountains in the background. They took a lot of pictures as a reminder of the beautifully colored wildflowers scattered about the landscape. They soon lost their way and were asking for directions to get back to the *Marco Polo.*

Mykonos, a Tiny Island in Greece
Rising Sharply out of the Aegean

Soon the group sailed to the island of Mykonos. Upon arrival, they boarded a tender that would take them to the well-known island, which they soon discovered to be dry and rugged. Ten miles long and seven miles wide, Mykonos is one of the smallest of the Cycladic group. Its two highest peaks are less than 1,197 feet above sea level. Legend has it that the rocks strewn across the barren landscape are the solidified remains of the giants slain by Hercules. Though it seemed deserted, the island had become one of the most popular and expensive of the Aegean islands. Many tourists enjoyed the sun and sunny beaches. On the beach, many beached boats were parked on the sand along the main promenade. The Greek islands seemed to rise sharply out of the Aegean, with narrow black beaches that created picturesque landscapes and were formed by centuries of eruptions. The travels viewed buildings built on slopes and many boats sitting nearby in the picturesque harbor.

They enjoyed their visit as they walked along the whitewashed streets to see the island's upscale bars and restaurants, cubical houses, and churches with light blue doors and domes. Glancing into the jewelry shop windows, they dragged their feet along the cobblestone streets. Nancy stopped along the way to make a phone call to the states, and Helen and Anna seemed to lose her somewhere in the area. They happily continued their walk and were soon drawn to the Greek wares in the tiny shops, again stopping to buy some jewelry.

The ride back to the *Marco Polo* was rough and wet, but they had to hurry and dress formally for their picture-taking session with the captain and to meet for cocktails and dinner. The next time they saw Nancy, she was safely onboard the ship, also busy getting ready for dinner. Champagne was served, and they were able to meet the officers of the ship. Again, the dinner at the Seven Seas, lobster this time, was simply wonderful, as was the music of the strolling Gypsy violinists.

After dinner, they enjoyed evening entertainment by a talented group of Marco Polo singers and dancers. The group proceeded to the library to play cards but soon heard the sounds of the slot machines dropping coins and giving out money. They needed to try their luck and quickly ended the card game, as the casinos were calling. Helen did win a little bit of money on the quarter and dollar machines. Weary from the hectic day, she headed for bed to dream about their morning arrival in Santorini.

From out of the Sea into a Wall
of Stone and a Part of
The Rim of a Massive Volcano
is the Island of Santorini

Bright and early, the group shared breakfast at Raffles with a lovely new friend named Dorothy. Upon their arrival in Santorini, they saw one of the Aegean's most spectacular sights. The southerly island immediately cast a magic spell, showing its archeological wealth that spanned the entire cultural history of the Aegean. Here the visitors took in dramatic landscapes and picturesque bays. The island appeared to rise up out of the sea into a wall of stone, a part of the rim of a massive volcano, which exploded in 1500 BC. Visually, Santorini was the most extraordinary sight in the Aegean, wherein the cliffs surrounded the flooded crater, rising 1,000 feet above the water's edge, with the towns of Fira and Ola perched above. The donkeys stood on the quay, waiting to carry the folks upward over sloping paths to a charming town, which could also be reached by cable car. They were unable to ride the donkeys, as there was a strike in progress. It was sad to know that many families had moved away after an earthquake in 1956 had left behind much destruction.

In this area, two large plates of the earth's crust met the African and Aegean plates. Santorini's soil was extremely fertile because of the volcano eruptions, which allowed all types of civilization to flourish there.

Port of Athinios and the Search for Atlantis

The group continued farther in their journey, taking the tender to the Port of Athinios, and thus began the search for Atlantis: "The Happy Isle Submerged by the Sea," according to Plato. Upon arriving at the port, they took a motor coach, soon reaching the site of Akrotiri. In about 2,500 BC, the eruption of the volcano buried the entire island, causing all traces of human activity to vanish for several centuries. With many warnings and several tremors, many people left the island. Many scholars believe that the lost Atlantis is Santorini itself. Walking around and learning some of the ancient history of this Minoan civilization was fascinating. These people had so much knowledge, proving their great intelligence at an early time in history. At the site, archeologists found three levels of concrete walls; windows; intact pottery; and painted walls in vibrant colors, depicting serpents, trees, and a sewer system for disposal of water.

Later, the group continued by bus, climbing steep hills, which enabled the travelers to see panoramic views of the bay, fruitful vineyards, and spinning windmills. The warm weather was also suitable for growing tomatoes, pistachio nuts, and many grapevines for the delicious wine. Thinking back, Helen realized the port was a reminder of a special place that is now lost in time.

They soon arrived at the town of Fiura, where they enjoyed wandering around the center of town within sight of the beautiful, azure blue bay. As usual, Helen was busy talking and walking that, when she noticed a sign that pointed to an older Catholic church nearby, she looked and followed the sign and, before long, missed a step. Falling down hard on the concrete walkway, she was embarrassed, helpless, and unable to get up on her own two feet. A very kind gentleman had been walking behind them and saw what had happened. He quickly offered his help, lifting her up in his strong arms and standing her up on her two feet. After a brief rest, Helen felt sore all over, although she continued to walk. After the fall and hurt feelings, the group visited and prayed at the quaint Catholic church building.

When the scenic tour was over, they rode the cable car down the mountain, enjoying more majestic views. It was regretful that they would miss riding down on the cute donkeys because of the strike. Hot and tired, they caught the tender back to the *Marco Polo*, their home away from home. They needed a little rest and looked forward to their delicious dinner waiting for them onboard the ship.

After another tasty dinner, they hurried off to see the evening's entertainment: Pat Mooney, Ireland's favorite comedy star. Later, the evening became even more interesting, as Helen and her friend Nancy visited the piano bar, where they met Ronald and Rosemary from the Berkshires. Happily, they accepted the offer to join them at the Charleston Lounge upstairs for disco dancing, where they got to dance with Ron. Very soon, Nancy was introduced to Chris, an engineer specialist for the cruise line. After the disco closed, and it was very late, Nancy invited Helen to sleep in her big bed and share her room. It was a good idea, as Helen would not have to disturb Anna and John.

Cruising along The Mediterranean Waters For a Day in Taormina, Sicily

After a good night's rest, with clothes and shoes in hand, Helen proceeded down the hall to her room to shower and dress. A lady passing down the hall called out to her, "I know what you were up to last night." Helen could only imagine what this strange lady was thinking and began laughing out loud, as it seemed very funny at the time. After a delightful breakfast, Helen and Anna took a few line dancing lessons. They learned additional steps to the electric slide, as well as taking in their morning exercise.

The *Marco Polo* was sailing to Taormina, Sicily, where the group would spend the whole day. The ship cruised on a beautiful, blue-green sea, which was very calm, along the Mediterranean, in waters 10,500 feet deep. The captain slowed down the ship by running on one engine, in order to delay their arrival in Taormina for early wake-up time.

During the day, the group stopped to watch the vegetable carving demonstration, which proved to be of major interest to Nancy and Anna. It wasn't long before they had to wake up Helen from her much-needed nap, as she was missing the beautiful classical concert at sea. The dinner was especially nice that evening. They could pretend they were in London at a famous restaurant, enjoying the scrumptious meal, which was duplicated with the permission of the Café Royale. They later enjoyed Marco Polo showtime with Jon Barker, who wrote and sang his own songs. The entertainment continued with "The Magical Illusions."

As soon as the entertainment was over, they wandered close to the slot machine area, and Helen began to hear the sweet music of the slot machines. Someone was winning, and in her mind, she could almost hear the slot machines calling. Helen continued to play the slots, while keeping her cool; she won some and lost some. Later on, it was time to head for the Charleston Club on another part of the ship, for the featured Sing along Pub Night and a trip down memory lane. Nancy and Helen stayed on for the disco dancing with Chris and Ron. Totally exhausted, they called it a night and set the clocks back one hour.

A View of the Mt. Etna Volcano
And Taormina, the Jewel of Sicily

As planned, the *Marco Polo* arrived at Taormina very early in the morning. After a tasty breakfast at Raffles, the group hurried to the top deck for a view of the smoking magnificence of Europe's Mt. Etna, the second highest volcano at 11,000 feet. Docking a short time later, they were about to enter Sicily, "the crossroads of the Mediterranean." You could picture almost half of the ancient civilized world of many nations as they came by ships and traveled across the dusty roads to get a good look.

Taormina, the Mediterranean's largest island, is known as the "Jewel of Sicily." Legend, mystery, myth, and magic meet you at every turn. The island is also known as the melting pot of the Mediterranean. It was very exciting to visit this island of scenic and historical splendor, where the travelers saw Greek temples, Roman ruins, Norman castles and churches, Arab and Byzantine domes, and splendid Baroque churches and palaces. Great imperial dynasties had left their stamp here among Taormina's mild climates and sweeping views. It was easy to imagine how life must have been here many years ago and to see it as we see it today.

Upon their arrival by tender, the group made their way into a small, picturesque town at the foot of the mountain in the Port Village of Naxos, where they visited quaint shops and soaked up the sun, walking along the tiny beach. After a fun shopping trip, they were beginning to feel the effects of the warm sun and decided to return to the cool air-conditioning on board the *Marco Polo* for some needed rest.

As they enjoyed the warm spa on deck, they had a clear picture of the active Mt. Etna volcano as it was sending out smoke signals across the magnificent Mediterranean. The entire trip seemed to be unbelievable and packed with much to see and do. They had a great time all evening, got a good night's sleep, and woke up to find that they were in another interesting and exciting foreign country.

Soon they were about to enter the Strait of Messina into Italy. The captain advised that a pilot captain of a small craft was coming on board to guide the *Marco Polo* through the channel heading for Sorrento. Helen recalled the old, famous song "Come Back to Sorrento."

After another wonderful dinner, it was show time in the Ambassador Lounge, where the Marco Polo singers and dancers gave a great tribute to Broadway. They were a very talented and enjoyable group.

View of the Stromboli Volcano Puffing Smoke Was Eagerly Watched, Exciting A Lot Of Folk

At about 10:30 p.m., the Captain notified the passengers to go on deck so they could view the eruption of the Stromboli volcano. The bright red volcano puffing smoke high up in the sky, lighting the way while the ship moved in the darkness at sea was a sight to see. After some brief, unforgettable, and exciting moments, the passengers returned to the lounge to enjoy the stylish Filipino Folkloric show. The native Filipinos performed in their traditional costumes, sharing their culture in song and dance with broad smiles on their faces. The performers were happy to be able to share their customs and lifestyle with the travelers on board. When the show was over, they hurried to the Charleston Club for the Late Night Cabaret to laugh along with the comedy routine. It wasn't too much later when the travelers were off to bed and were soon out like a light. Dreamland was soothing, and getting some much-needed sleep and rest felt good.

Sorrento, Italy, in a Sheltered Isle With Luxuriant Hills, Mile per Mile

By morning, the *Marco Polo* arrived in Sorrento, and the group had a good breakfast at Raffles, while looking out at the scenic view from the ship. Many homes were nestled up in the hills, overlooking the beautiful, azure waters.

Sorrento, with grapevines, olives, and quality fruit trees, is situated on a tract of coastline of unrivaled beauty in a sheltered isle surrounded by luxuriant hills, reminding Helen of the song "Come Back to Sorrento." The town looked down over the port, which featured two marinas. Ocean access to the island's roads consisted of very steep stairs and narrow passageways, carved into the rock. Legend has it that the name *Sorrento* is poetically dated back to the sirens who lived in the rocks on the gulf.

Many times, the sirens would try in vain to ensnare Ulysses with their deadly song, and it seemed Ulysses always strapped himself to the mast of his ship, looking the other way as he sailed past this fatal place. Upon arrival in Sorrento, the group took the tender, continuing to Marina de Capri and transferred to an air-conditioned jet boat.

Such a Feeling to Be Free at the Isle of Capri With Tranquility and Peace Don't You Agree

They quickly boarded their bus, which drove up to a magnificent, well-known area at the Isle of Capri and another beautiful view, at 1,500 feet above sea level. As their eyes traveled far and wide, they could see the boats, which looked like tiny toys that were scattered everywhere into the sea. The ride on the chairlift took them to Anna Capri, which is a community for the wealthy and elite of Italy. They eagerly visited a very expensive shop that featured Capodimonte statues and the like, which were made in Italy. They looked over some famous fashion brands from all over the world, including inlaid furniture and a large selection of Armani porcelain statues and lamps.

Another place they visited was a very famous museum, Villa An Michele. They were told that when a Swedish doctor, who had lived in an old Roman villa in Capri, died, he left his entire state to the Swedish government. The museum consisted of some furniture, pictures, and many beautiful gardens, revealing an older type of lifestyle, and everything was preserved for others to enjoy. The group had a very pleasant time, walking and touring the very expensive and quaint shops they found along the way.

They laughed as they watched the mode of transportation in use: a cable car called a Funicolare in Italy, and Helen remembered hearing the word in songs in the past. It was fun to put the two together, and actually see a Funicolare in action. They learned that neither cars nor busses were allowed in certain areas, as the people were very concerned with pollution caused by motor fuel. Furniture was being moved about in a wooden box situated on top of a small motor scooter. You could imagine what a fiasco it would be to move a large houseful of heavy furniture. The group hated to leave this peaceful and unique place, but it was fun to ride the Funicolare back down to the bus. After the tour, they boarded the new, air-conditioned jet boat for the ride back to the *Marco Polo*.

Once on board, they headed to the top deck to enjoy the spa and warm sun for a quiet hour of rest and comfort. After another evening champagne reception, hosted by their captain at poolside, they enjoyed a delicious dinner, which was followed with baked Alaska as a special treat for dessert.

Later, it was off to the Ambassador Lounge for variety show time, and the group continued the night at the Charleston Club, disco dancing into the wee hours. The group was tired and welcomed their sleep time, as they dreaded the 5:45 a.m. wake-up call for their trip into Rome.

Port of Civitavecchia in Romantic Rome
They're in No Big Hurry to Get Back Home

After a light breakfast, the pilot ship led them through the main port of Rome. As the group disembarked, they quickly headed toward the tour bus, traveling fifty miles to continue on a tour of Rome. Driving past the port, they rode past the two thousand-year-old Michelangelo Fort. It was to their benefit (and interesting to note) that the Roman Administration did not require the bus driver to pay any tolls for the roads, as they wanted to encourage the flow of tourist money to help the poor.

The group was informed that many of the trees drained the swamps, and this was nature's way to get rid of the mosquitoes. Not only did Rome's rich soil produce delicious grapes, it ensured that the longhorn cattle had good grazing land as well.

After stopping at a rest stop for some lunch, the group learned of an Italian custom practiced in the restaurants. It was proper to first pay for the food and get a receipt, and very soon another restaurant worker would follow with the food order. The person handling the food, they learned, was unable to collect the money at the same time, which made a lot of sense.

They stopped for lunch, and while on their way, they crossed the bridge over the Tiber River. Helen could almost picture the Roman soldiers marching over the river as they had done many thousands of years earlier. A bit farther on, they saw the ancient ruins, the only pyramid in Rome, and Aventine Hill. As they rode farther, they were off to Circus Maximus and Seven Hills of Ancient Rome, along roads of hard-to-walk on cobblestone. Their next stop was a bit eerie—they toured the two thousand-year-old Colosseum, where the gladiators fought the ferocious lions while over fifty thousand spectators watched.

They briefly visited St. Mary's Church, one of the largest of eighty churches in Rome and dedicated to the Virgin Mary. Many years ago they found snow on the hill, and it became known as the Church of the Snow. Their visit included a stop at the very famous Trevi Fountain, which was incredibly beautiful and had been built in 1762. For many years, there had been an old saying—"if you throw three coins in the fountain and make three wishes, they possibly might come true." Helen had stopped at the Trevi Fountain several years before, and one of her wishes had been to return to the romantic city of Rome. It was almost hard to believe that she was back a few years later and would once again cast a few coins in the magic fountain with new wishes. Helen always liked to think that life was another adventure in time, and she wondered whether she would return for a third time, possibly for a romantic interlude.

Rome has always been known as the city of fountains, and rightfully so. Later on, the group stopped at the Bernini Bristol Hotel for lunch, where they met and sat with their new companion, Liz from Las Vegas Their Italian lunch was a superb combination of pasta, veal, and a dish of the sweetest strawberries they had ever tasted. Company at the lunch table was fascinating when Liz joined the group and captured their attention with great conversation. She, too, was an avid reader of *The Spotlight* newspaper and had lots of news to share with the group. As they came out of the Bernini Bristol Hotel, they found the streets had cooled down and were wet with rain. Their bus was waiting and ready to continue the tour.

The group hurried on to the bus, which soon drove past the American Embassy, a very beautiful palace on Via Veneto Street, and past the Excelsior Hotel (very expensive and famous). They also passed some ancient walls that had been built to protect the Roman soldiers; it was a clear symbol of the fall of the Roman Empire.

Upon leaving Rome, they saw the ancient Justice Palace of Rome and Santangelo.

The tour also stopped for picture taking and street shopping, and Helen bought a black scarf and tote bag to take home as a souvenir. Soon the long awaited moment had arrived: They entered the State of the Vatican City, the smallest city-state in the entire world, at St. Peter's Square. Upon entering St. Peter's Basilica, the group noticed the many large statues that appeared to be on guard all along the top colonnade. They saw the Chapel of the Pieta, which Michelangelo made at the young age of twenty-four. This was a representation of the Sorrow of Madonna holding her dead son and displaying her acceptance of the will of God. This was the only statue he ever signed. They admired the beautiful mosaic work as they looked up at the ceiling. Looking around in all directions, they saw such incredible beauty, and their visit to the church was indescribable. Standing and walking about, they could feel the spirit in every corner of the room with a great sense of inner peace. Once again, they stopped to shop near the church, where Helen bought crosses on a gold chain designed by the pope for Linda and Ann to have as a special reminder of this remarkably holy place.

As Helen and Ann waited for their tour bus, they barely survived crossing the Via della Conciliazione Street, because of the heavy traffic and crazy drivers. Honking of horns was not permitted, and the brave people took a big chance as they made their way across the street, and they would get in front of the cars to make a run for it. All the while Helen and Ann prayed deep down inside that they would not be run over by the speeding traffic. Luckily, they made it to the next pit stop, where they searched desperately for a much-needed bathroom. On their way, they found a restaurant at downstairs level, where they met with another surprise. As Helen came out of the bathroom stall, she noticed two men waiting for the stalls, and she exclaimed out loud, "Am I in the wrong place?"

Just then, Anna came out and said the exact same thing. Funny, they had the same thoughts; both found openly sharing their restrooms with strange men to be another new experience on their trip to the city of Rome.

While standing in line waiting for the tour bus, Anna was busy speaking in Russian to a Sicilian couple as they waited for *their* tour bus. They were very surprised to meet and speak with the strangers in their native Russian while visiting Rome. As the tour bus pulled in, the very handsome Sicilian gentleman asked Helen if he could give her a little kiss on both cheeks, as was the custom of the Russian people. So Helen got her Russian kisses from the Sicilian gentleman on a Roman street in broad daylight as the gentleman happily waved his good-byes with the arrival of his bus.

On their trip, Helen and Anna noticed the reactions of the people in many of the foreign countries toward Americans visiting their lands. They were warm, friendly, and kind to everyone. The tour bus finally arrived, and the travelers boarded, ready to start their long ride to the Port of Civitavecchia. The group was tired, and as they neared the *Marco Polo*, they could hear the beautiful sounds of music in the distance, welcoming them back to the ship. It was so thoughtful of some of the Roman people to greet them with a thirty piece navy band and many lovely young ladies bringing beautiful fresh flowers. This was a great welcome and a heartwarming, first-time experience for the group as they boarded their ship.

On board, they were tired and hungry and eagerly looked forward to their dinner, which was waiting, as they'd missed their early dinner seating.

They knew they would use their time wisely and headed for the casino, as they heard bells ringing and the slot machines calling. They decided to try their luck for a short time but were soon disappointed, and exhausted from their long trip, they went to bed early to dream about tomorrow's adventure.

Livorno, Italy, with Romantic Canals
A Meeting Place for the Guys and Gals

Saturday, a bright and sunny morning, the *Marco Polo* docked at the dynamic city of Livorno. This impressive city was developed around the port, which was home to a lot of commercial activity, industry, and crafts. Livorno was located in the heart of the quarter known as Piccola Venezia, known for the romantic canals coursing through the city. The Fortezza-Nuova is protected by a complete moat. This great work was finished by the Medici family. There was a well-maintained public garden and scenic park, which they were anxious to see.

After a very early breakfast, the group left the ship. As they passed the Foretzza-Nuova on the way into the city, it was fun to stop and visit several of the local shops and interesting street markets. There was a slight problem with the money situation—the banks were closed, as it was Saturday. They, nevertheless, managed to buy some trinkets to take back home as souvenirs. They were careful with the handling of their money, and Helen made a small chart of lira versus US dollars. It came in handy when the ladies bargained with the vendors. The girls called a cab to get back to their very comfortable floating hotel after Nancy stopped for some Italian ice cream.

It was good to relax, rest a bit, and enjoy the excellent food served at Raffles. They spent the rest of the afternoon sitting in the spa on deck for a short time and sunbathing while taking in the luxury of the cool, blue waters on such a pleasant day. At 3:00 p.m., they went to Raffles to enjoy tea and cakes with their friends.

Later in the evening, they feasted at the Café Royale for dinner and were soon off to enjoy *Marco Polo* show time. For a short time, they joined the others at the piano bar. Helen and Nancy were soon off to the Charleston Club for disco dancing. Stopping off at the piano bar, they invited Ron to join them for some good dancing. At 2:00 a.m., they all said good night and were off to bed.

PORTOFINO, ITALY, A NARROW INLET
IN THE HEART OF THE ITALIAN RIVIERA

Hardly containing their excitement as they entered Portofino, they could see the beautiful harbor and pine-covered hillsides, with elegant boutiques and chic cafés that overlooked the small, picturesque, jewel-like bay. Portofino may be the most famous small port in the world. Secluded and exclusive, the tiny village has long been the holiday home and playground for many of the rich and famous. Today yachts, almost the size of the *Marco Polo*, filled the harbor with beautiful buildings that are neatly set back in the hills. It is interesting to note that Portofino's roots go back to the Roman times. Finally in 1935, Genoa took over the government of the village, declaring it a national monument. It may be a good thing that very little has changed for the past sixty years.

After the tender dropped them off at the port, they were able to enjoy the expensive shops. Helen bought some postcards and a black lace fan. After they got back to the *Marco Polo*, they changed for the spa on the upper deck, where they intended to relax and enjoy the sun and fresh air.

The excitement mounted as they were to arrive early in the evening at Cannes, France. They went aboard the boat on a cool night, and it sped through the water toward Cannes.

Cannes, Well Known as the Pearl in France Playing at the Casinos, Almost in a Trance

They boarded a bus and soon met an interesting man named Steve, who had a business in Cannes but lived in Ft. Lauderdale, Florida. It would seem that he enjoyed his work and often traveled to far away places. The crowded city soon came in to view and seeing it so beautifully lit up was nice. Since it was the last day of a film festival, many famous movie stars were enjoying the celebration. The excitement was everywhere as the group entered the Croisette Casino and changed their US dollars for some French francs. Helen got busy playing two slot machines with French francs for a short time, and seeing French words like *marche* seemed strange. It wasn't very long before the group noticed the bells were not ringing. This could only mean that the slots were not paying. Helen needed help and made polite conversation with an English-speaking merchant seaman, who was playing the machines. He kindly helped her with the slot machine and then asked what time she would be back tomorrow so they could get together. It seemed funny, as Helen had told the gentleman she didn't know where she would be in Cannes tomorrow, and she thanked him for his kindness.

After a fun-filled evening, the group caught the bus back to the waiting tender, making their way back to the *Marco Polo*. The boat ride was short and exhilarating in the cool night air as the waves splashed their faces.

Upon returning to the *Marco Polo*, they found their friends waiting at the piano bar, and soon they were off to the disco for nighttime dancing.

After total exhaustion had overcome them, they gave in to sleepy time and headed for bed.

Cannes and Monte Carlo Known for High Society And the World-famous Playground of the Stars

Up bright and early, the group had a quick breakfast, disembarked, and searched for a waiting bus. They would be making an exciting journey, through Cannes and Monte Carlo, with 1,200,000 inhabitants, and most famous for its annual film festival in May. The city turns into a star-studded kaleidoscope of elegant boutiques, ritzy hotels, fine restaurants, casinos, chic nightclubs, and sprawling estates. In 1834, Cannes was once a Roman settlement, attracting the British and the rich and sophisticated from Europe and allowing for 129 different citizenships.

The French Riviera stretched along the Mediterranean coast of France from Toulon to the Italian border with its vast expanse of beaches, many boat slips, and warm weather. Along the Riviera, blooms of mimosa, wisteria, oleander, and bougainvillea set fire to the hills for a perfect haven.

The group continued, traveling through Antibes, with a harbor that is the center of Mediterranean yachting and a look at the sixteenth-century Fort Carre.
They were able to see where Napoleon was once imprisoned as they followed the scenic coastline past the Hippodrome and its sixteenth-century castle built by the Grimaldi family. Picasso spent five months here creating works, such as his incomparable "La Joie de Vivre."

As the group traveled farther, they realized that the fishermen were putting out too many nets into the sea. This became a serious problem, as they were running out of fish. Driving along they could see farms made in the sea, where fishermen grew fish, enabling them to harvest their fish crops in two years.

Nice, the Capital of the French Riviera And Well-Known "Goddess of Victory"

The group arrived at Nice, the capital of the French Rivera, where they viewed colorful markets and striking modern architecture. Nice was a well-known, busy trading center. They visited a war memorial at the top of the hill facing the harbor where many names of dead US soldiers who had participated in the Second World War were etched. They stopped briefly to take pictures. For a short time, they traveled from Nice to Monaco.

Monaco, Glittering Capital of Monte Carlo, The Second Smallest City-State in the World

Passing the grandstands of the Grand Prix and continuing on through several tunnels, they soon arrived in Monte Carlo via the Corniche Moyenne. Governed by Prince Ranier III, Monte Carlo was an independent principality. It had started as a Greek settlement and then had become Roman. The Grimaldi family purchased Monaco in 1309 from the Genoese. For seven hundred years, the Grimaldi family had controlled the oldest monarchy in the world. The treaty with France would guarantee the country's continued independence as long as a Grimaldi occupied the throne.

In Monte Carlo, a glittering administrative area in Monaco, the rich and famous gathered year after year to gamble at the Grand Casino and bask in the sun. Because of the casino, which was created by the founder of Monte Carlo, citizens of Monaco did not have to pay any taxes and continued to enjoy the highest per capita income in the world. Of the 31,000 people who lived there, 25,000 residents were international. The French made their own stamps, with tourism as their main industry. There was hardly any crime in the area, and travelers were told the policy was to "shoot on sight" if anyone was caught stealing.

In order to get up to Monaco, the group had to take an escalator and a lift. An upset woman told them that, while she was on the lift, someone had pushed her, and she later noticed that her beautiful gold bracelet had been taken off her wrist. It should be noted that Monaco-Ville sits on a hill called the Rock. When first arriving at the top of the hill, the travelers could see the Jacques Cousteau Museum, but they were unable to stop in and take a look at the many rare species of marine plants and animals. They visited the Palais de Prince, the Grand Italianate Palace, facing a large square. They looked to see if the flag was flying, which meant that the prince was in the castle, and they were unable to visit. At noon, they heard the ringing of the bells, which preceded the changing of the guard. This was a daily ceremony performed by the prince's French Carabinieri in their dazzling white uniforms.

The group enjoyed a tasty lunch outdoors at Monaco-Ville in Freddy's International French Restaurant. With a little time on their hands, the group bought some gifts and postcards for mailing to their friends and families at home. They were soon off to the Hotel de Paris.

The group then stopped off at the Carlo Hotel and Casino. Helen quickly went to the restaurant across the way to change her US dollars into French francs so she could gamble in the casino. She quickly won over 300 francs (60.00 US dollars). Since they were on tour, they had to leave in a hurry, and unhappily, Helen had to stop winning. What a shame!

The Corniche Moyene followed the old Roman Via Aurelia route built by Napoleon. It was still one of the most beautiful highways in the world, affording travelers incomparable views of the Mediterranean coastline as it snaked around the high mountain cliffs that plunged into the sea. On a bright, sunny morning you could see Corsica, 9,000 feet from the road to Monaco. They passed the City of Eze, one of the Riviera's most famous villas, rising 1,400 feet above the sea and commanding a magnificent view of the surrounding area.

On their way back to Cannes and the waiting *Marco Polo* by bus, the group was surprised to see people sunbathing topless on the beach. Their short bus ride soon brought them back to the tender and their awaiting ship.

On board, they all met for an enjoyable time for tea and cakes. After another delicious dinner, the group met up with Ron and Rose Mary at the Polo Lounge for show time, and sharing drinks, jokes, and easy conversation, they had a wonderful time. Later on, they went up to the Charleston Club for late disco dancing for the young at heart. Even Anna and John decided to join the disco group. Earlier in the day before in

Cannes they had met a nice man on the bus from Ft. Lauderdale, and he invited Helen to dance, which was a lot of fun. Too soon it was off to bed so they could dream about tomorrow and Spain.

Palma De Mallorca, One of Spain's Treasures, Makes a Life Here Full of Tropical Pleasures

Following a quick breakfast at Raffles, the group was off to visit fascinating Spain. They arrived in Palma, amidst swaying palms; cedars; and olive, orange, lemon, and fig trees. The city shone in glory, with a turquoise sky, a sea of blue, and emerald mountains. This allowed the people to wear light summer clothes to handle the burning heat. For the past one hundred fifty years, millions of tourist postcards have echoed a view of life in Mallorca. It is the largest of the Balearic Islands, which began some fifty-seven miles off Alicante on the Spanish Coast, extending northeast into the Mediterranean Sea. Upon arriving in Palma, you can see Palma's Gothic Cathedral and other ancient monuments in the distance.

A bus was waiting to take the disembarking group into the city, where the travelers could look around and do some shopping. It seemed strange to get on the bus, hold open your hand, and tell the bus driver to take as many coins as he needed. The money was different, and they felt helpless, placing their trust in complete strangers. With the receipt of their ticket, they were soon on their way. Their adventure in this busy city was impressive, as well as exciting. After a long wait in the hot weather at the bus stop, they made the return trip to the *Marco Polo*.

They hated to miss their scheduled teatime but were glad to arrive in time for their usually wonderful dinner. In a short while, it was time to go to the upper deck to view the performance of a talented, young Spanish group from Barcelona, who sang and danced for the captive audience. The orchestra was great. and Helen had her last dance with Ron. Sadly, they had to prepare to leave the ship in the morning, and they placed their luggage in the hall for pickup at midnight.

Visit Barcelona, Spain's Richest City
To Miss The Architecture Would Be A Pity

After a hearty breakfast at Raffles, the group was off to the Ambassador Lounge to wait for the custom agents to board the *Marco Polo*. The group headed for Barcelona on a four- hour tour, which proved to be interesting and very exhausting. It was a little sad because the time had come to say adios to their new friends, Nancy, Ron, Rose Mary, and Liz.

Barcelona, an ultra-modern financial district, was an immense shopping area with unique architecture and a multitude of first-rate sightseeing spots. When the work was done at the end of the day, the people could depart from the Diagonal and go on to the Golden Block, where they could walk past some of the most celebrated Art Nouveau buildings, including the Batillo House. They also saw the Sagrada Famili Cathederal, which was one of Gaudi's unfinished most recognized landmarks. It offered the greatest display of twenty-ninth century architecture in the world. Barcelona's high cost of living caused many young people to move to little villages. The group traveled the tour on Via Latetana, where they saw lots of motorcycles in the city (two hundred thousand bikes). Helen was reminded a bit of bike week in Daytona Beach and the bike traffic the local people had to deal with.

The guide told the group that social security was free for the people, but she feared there would not be any benefits left for her when she retired. She mentioned that many of the young people were not having children because they were unable to afford them.
While driving along the streets, the group noticed that many of the buildings were designed with broken tiles. Children were being taught four languages, namely Spanish, French, English, and Catalan.

Their rest stop included a visit to the Spanish Village, allowing the travel group to visit quaint shops along the narrow cobblestone streets. After passing the Arenas de Barcelona (the old bullfight arena), they went on to Gran Via.

After a very interesting tour, the bus arrived at the Hilton Hotel. Helen, Anna, and John settled in their room then went to the restaurant for a tasty

Spanish meal, which cost muchas pesetas. Helen noticed a man reading his daily newspaper with what looked like a very large rolling pin inside. She asked him about the long-looking rolling pin, and he replied that he found it easier to read his cumbersome paper in that way. Their stay at the Hilton in the heat of downtown Barcelona was a pleasant one. They had an opportunity to finish their shopping in the large department stores. The elegant clothes and shoes in the windows were beautiful and very well made. They noticed that the people liked to dress up for work. While shopping, patrons were offered candy and treats and the department stores permitted dogs. They seemed to have different customs, didn't they?

Later, the bus took them to the airport, and the trio was on their way home via Iberia Airlines. They changed planes in Madrid, went through customs, then waited for their plane to JFK in New York. Helen and Anna continued searching for souvenirs but quickly found out they were unable to get past a certain door. As they tried to open the door, the guard threatened them with the Policia. They rushed back in a hurry because they didn't want to get left behind and go to a Spanish jail for opening the forbidden door.

Safely on the plane at last, they had a seven-hour flight, arriving at Kennedy Airport in New York. Luckily, they quickly found their luggage, as they found the busy airport was like a zoo. It was nice to have their limo driver waiting to take them to Anna and John's home in New Jersey. This gave Helen some rest after her memorable trip before it was time for her to catch another plane to Daytona Beach.

Some Time to Retire to Enjoy Each Fun-filled Day, Watching the Sunrises and Sunsets Along the Way

After Helen returned from her fun-filled adventure to the Mediterranean, she decided it was time to retire from the real estate profession and travel the world. She wanted to enjoy many more trips, with lots of time for pleasure. The time had come to sell her real estate business and office complex and make plans to travel around the world.

It was only a month into her retirement when Helen met Len at Oceans Seven Condo at the beach. A recently retired New York City commissioner,

Len had moved to Daytona so he could look after his parents, as his father had recently been diagnosed with cancer.

Helen and Len spent a lot of time enjoying the beach with the hot sand tickling their feet as they waded through the waves. They swam, walked, and fed the birds on the beach. Helen bought an oceanfront condo, unit 1003, on the tenth floor. A year later, Helen bought another unit, 1502, with a river view, and Len bought a condo as well. It was time for Anna and John to leave New Jersey and become Florida residents in their early retirement. They liked the ocean condo life and traded their seasonal home in A Quiet Place in the Country for Helen's riverfront condo. Helen moved to unit 1406 and did a lot of work remodeling the condo, which finished up beautifully. From the balcony of the condo, you could look down at the ocean and river with magnificent views of the sunrise and sunset.
Nancy soon came on board, selling her home in A Quiet Place in the Country and buying a condo unit in the building. Living in one building at Oceans Seven was really a lot of fun for the three sisters.

Within a short period of time, Len's father passed away, and his mom, Anna, moved from her home in Ormond Beach. She bought unit 1405. This was a better arrangement, as Len could more easily check on her. Len was soon voted in as the president of the association of Oceans Seven, and Helen was voted in as secretary. They controlled five votes and were able to take part in the betterment of Oceans Seven. Living there with all their family and friends was a lot of fun. The family, Len, and his mother would all meet for drinks and treats at Helen's condo, enjoying cocktail time instead of tea at "teatime."

In August 1998, Helen took a trip with Len's mom, Anna, for a short visit to their families in New Jersey. It was exciting to visit some of the casinos in Atlantic City. The women did their share of gambling and won a little money at the slot machines. After their visit, where they each enjoyed quality time with their families, it was time to head back to Florida.

A surprise hurricane seemed to appear out of nowhere as they approached a quiet Georgia town. It was an eerie feeling as Len drove his van into the nearest gas station. They were surprised to find the whole town in darkness without any electricity and no gas available at the pump. Len kept his cool and drove, heading south and looking for the next town. It was fun to get away, but returning home felt good.

How to Avoid the Shark Bites at Daytona Beach With Some Lessons Jay Jay Knows How to Teach

Sometime in 1999, while watching television, Helen looked up and saw Jay Jay being interviewed on TV news. They lived close to the beach and this enabled him to enjoy surfing at the beach, especially when the waves were rough. He was a good surfer and watched carefully for sharks in the water. One day while he was surfing, his foot was bitten by a shark, and he forgot to tell his mother about it. Helen could see where the shark had bitten his foot, causing him to get stitches. When questioned further, Jay Jay said he would continue to surf in the ocean and was not afraid of the possibility of dangerous shark bites. Naturally, it was a surprise to Helen to see and hear about this for the first time on TV.

Cruising the Grand Cayman, Playa Del Carmen, Cozumel, Mexico, the Mississippi, and New Orleans

A cruise to Mexico aboard the *Carnival Sensation* from Tampa Bay in May 2000 was fun and relaxing. Their expectations of fine dinners and entertainment were eagerly met with a taste for the good life.

Their first stop was the Grand Cayman Islands, which is located about one hundred miles south of Cuba in the Caribbean Sea and was discovered by Christopher Columbus in 1503. It was taken over by the British in about 1670. Georgetown, with a coral reef coastline, low elevation, and natural harbors is the capital. English is the official language, and banking interests are the chief economic activities.

After an early breakfast, they rushed to ride the tender to get to shore. Carefully, they boarded the glass-bottom boat for a look at life under the sea. Beautiful underwater marine gardens, rainbows of colorful fish, and a sunken cargo ship were visible as they looked down into the water.

Later, the group was able to get a free sample of black coral as they took a nice walk about the shops. Rum cake and a liter of liquor were the purchases of the day.

After a delightful lunch, the sailing hotel continued, en route to Mexico. After taking some nice photos, the group heard Lady Luck calling to them from the casino, where the slots rang up the money.

At 5:30 a.m., the phone rang, and after a quick breakfast buffet, they hurried to wait.

Their tender arrived, and they were off to Playa Del Carmen and their bus, and Pablo. Their bus took them to Cozumel, Mexico, and the Mayan Ruins. They learned that the Maya were the first people of the New World who kept written historical records; in 50 BC they began to inscribe texts on pots, bones, and palace walls. In 1511, on the way to Cuba, the Spaniards arrived here after being blown off course by a hurricane. The group made a visit to Tulum, which stands on a cliff overlooking the Caribbean. They learned that the priests married into families and that the deformed people had a special place in society and became very important. Corn was sacred and was placed in the mouth of the poor at burial for the next life; the Maya believed that the different colors of corn represented different colors of people around the world.

Later in the day, after a scenic ride, the group arrived at the waiting boat in Cozumel to see Old World Europe, with gas lanterns, cobblestone streets, horse-drawn carriages, and a feeling of Paris.

New Orleans and the Famous French Quarter

The group spent a very pleasant day aboard ship as they kept busy with many fun-filled activities. The next morning after breakfast, they were on their way to New Orleans. It was a good opportunity for Helen and Nancy to make a dash and try their luck at the casinos. It was interesting to watch the barges being loaded during the night, as they sailed along the muddy Mississippi River. Their experienced pilot carefully guided the cruise ship into the New Orleans Harbor, which is the second largest port in the United States.

In the morning after breakfast, the group boarded the bus that would take them on the anticipated city tour. They were told that the fearless Spanish explorers were the first Europeans to go to the lower Mississippi valley in 1530. They were a lively mix of Canadian frontiersmen, artisans, troops, convicts, and black and Indian Slaves. Reminiscent of Old World Europe with gas lanterns, cobblestone streets, and horse-drawn carriages, the French Quarter made the visit somewhat like a trip to Paris. Around the city, the area was dotted with elegant plantations, true to a very romantic, bygone era. The population of 1.2 million spoke Creole and some French and Spanish as well. The French Quarter was a charming area of sprawling, southern-style, Victorian homes; Italian court- yards; fountains; and ornate wrought-iron grillwork. The group stopped to look at the architecture of aboveground tombs in various style marbles, brick, and stucco. The crypts resembled small row houses or Greek-inspired temples made of marble. As the average elevation of the city was five feet below sea level, underground burial was impossible.

They went along Lake Pont-Chartrain and visited the city's fine yacht harbor, and then on to the old town of Carrolton to St. Charles Avenue, where they followed the streetcar to see many beautifully restored mansions. The Superdome, a gleaming saucer-shaped futuristic building and the home of the New Orleans Saints football team, could seat up to a hundred thousand people. The group continued their walk down St. Peter Street, where Tennessee Williams wrote *A Streetcar Named Desire*. The oldest continuously operating street railway system in existence, New Orleans's most famous mode of transportation was considered to be a moveable museum.

They group traveled to Jackson Square in the heart of the French Quarter, wherein local artists displayed works of art. In City Park, they found the Orleans Museum of Art. The park itself was a 1,500-acre expanse, with ancient live oaks; an amusement park with an antique, wooden carousel in a fairytale theme park; a ten-acre botanical garden; tennis courts; four golf courses; and eight miles of lagoons, featuring graceful swans and ducks, boating, fishing, and bird watching.

You can try your luck in one of the city casinos or take a horse-driven carriage ride through the downtown area. It seemed a little strange to see horses and mules wearing diapers to help keep the city clean. The group toured with fascinating interest the endless variety of sights in America's most European city. Stopping in one of the shops, they bought some beautifully designed masks and beads for later festivities.

Helen and Len toured Bourbon Street, stopping at the famous Café du Monde for a beignet, a square-shaped donut minus the hole dusted with powdered sugar. They stopped for a beer during their long walk, searching out the shops and feeling the city's ambiance. Hopping on a scenic ride on the trolley, they made their way to the harbor and the waiting ship.

Once aboard, they hastily ate dinner, anxious to be off to the Mardi Gras ship party. The partygoers danced to loud music in a carnival atmosphere, wearing masks and beads.

Up at 5:30 a.m. and off to an early breakfast, the group headed to the Plaza Lounge for their scheduled trip through customs. Upon arriving on shore, they met with the waiting cab driver, and it was time to go home to Daytona Beach.

Linda and Peter become Man and Wife, As They Eagerly Start their New Life

On July 15, 2000, Linda and Peter were married at the First United Methodist Church in Winter Park. The wedding reception, held at the Orlando Marriott Downtown Hotel, was special. Linda and Peter made a quick getaway for a wonderful honeymoon in the islands.

A few years later, they built a lovely home in Orlando.

On January 6, 2001, Helen's family was saddened when her older sister, Mary, passed away from cancer. Mary would always be in their thoughts, and the family would all miss her.

Three condos and three years later, Helen and Len grew tired of the continuing rising assessments and stringent rules at their condos, and it was time to move again. Helen, Len, and his mother, Anna, sold their condos and made their way to Spruce Creek. Len bought a home for his mom at Spruce Creek. Helen moved back to her home at #4 Lazy Eight Drive. where she quickly put her home up for sale.

A year later, as Helen was driving around Spruce Creek, she saw an older home on the golf course on Spruce Creek Boulevard. The price seemed fair and she liked the home and immediately bought it. Helen was ready for a new undertaking and would enjoy working on another endeavor. There were panoramic views of the golf course from all of the rooms and magnificent oak trees. After three months of completely remodeling the older model home, she was ready to make her move.

On May 25, 2001, their dear sweet friend and brother-in-law, Walter, passed away as a result of congestive heart failure. Sadly, Helen's family was getting older, and Walter would be missed. During the time when he was ill in the house, he kept himself busy making tapes for the entire family. He was great at adding to the tapes to make them more personal. Today, the family enjoys the tapes as they fondly think of him when they are played.

Len kept Helen busy as they traveled around visiting many places in Florida and checking out many quaint restaurants for dinner. Many evenings after dinner, Helen and Len would head to Barnes and Noble coffee shop and bookstore, where they would catch up on reading magazines. They'd look through some of the books, while enjoying some delicious coffee, tea, or cocoa. It almost seemed like they were visiting the library, where they were able to sit and read books, as well as choose to buy some they liked. It's wonderful to have the world at your fingertips as you travel through the magic world of books.

Helen and Len's friends, Gary and Rosemary from St. Augustine, would drive the long distance to Daytona Beach to talk and drink their favorite coffee. Len and Helen had met Gary and Rosemary couple of years earlier on a short sightseeing trip to St. Augustine. Helen had seen a window full of Armani figurines at the couple's shop, Cathedral Galleries. She was interested in a lady figurine seated at the piano. She bought the Armani, and their friendship began, and while they were waiting for them to become available, they would assist them in their shop.

Soon after, Rosemary and Gary made an important decision to sponsor a two-day event for charity, as well as for the opportunity to revisit with their clientele. Mr. Armani was coming all the way from Italy to St. Augustine to meet and greet the people at Rosemary's shop. He drew a sketch in front of everyone and then began to mold a magnificent sculpture, which was truly a work of art. The sculpture was auctioned off for twenty-five thousand dollars, and the money was given to charity.

The next morning, special arrangements were made for Helen and Len to be seated at Mr. Armani's table with his interpreters and officers for the company at the Casa Monica Hotel for brunch. Being close to this talented artist was very special to Helen. She had been a collector of his great works for over twenty years. It was so wonderful to know that he was visiting from Italy. As he visited with Helen and Len, they had his undivided attention. Mr. Armani explained that at home in Florence, Italy, he would sit and listen to music and create his magnificent statues and paint. He told Helen there would not be any more paintings. It was a great feeling to be sitting and chatting with Mr. Armani. a famous artist and a down-to-earth person.

Logan, with Bright Smile and Twinkling Eyes Almost Reminds Us of the Wondrous Skies

Jay Jay met Carrie, a truly beautiful young lady. Through their love, they were blessed with a wonderful son, Logan Thomas Erik, on March 26, 2001. Carrie, a wonderful young lady with lots of patience, was truly suited for Jay Jay; they seemed to belong together.

Tragedy struck New York City on September 11, 2001. The event would affect the lives of Americans forever, as our country was under attack by suicide bombers. Terrorists flew two commercial planes full of passengers directly into the Twin Towers in the World Trade Center buildings in New York City, leaving behind death and destruction. Thousands of innocent people were killed, and the buildings were destroyed. It was a scene from a horror movie, with people running for their lives from the smoke and fire.

Many firemen and policemen gave their lives that day as they tried to assist those trapped in the fire. Unbelievably, at the same time, a third commercial airliner was hijacked; the passengers on board bravely tried to divert the plane from the White House in Washington, DC, and. the legend of "Let's roll" was heard around the world. Sadly the plane went down in Shanksville, Pennsylvania, and all the brave people on board were killed.

Our Brave Military Men Get Ready for War

Intelligence agencies in the United States advised Americans to face the reality that Iraq was in possession of weapons of mass destruction and that its leadership had previously used poison gas to kill many of their own people. In March 2003, the United States, England, and other countries joined in the fight to stop the development of these weapons of mass destruction and prevent them from spreading throughout the world.

How Difficult it Must Surely Be,
Leaving Family, Friends and Me
Putting their Very Lives In Peril
and Facing a World in Turmoil

As the troops were leaving for Iraq, TV reporters watched the National Guard, parting with their families and bravely heading off to war. This was the beginning of the nation's news coverage of the war, as the media would follow the brave soldiers in Iraq.

After serving three years in military service in the army and surfing in Hawaii, Jay Jay was deployed. In December 2003, he left with the Florida National Guard to fight in Iraq. Crews of television reporters saw the group off as families cried and said their good-byes. This was the beginning of the nation's news coverage, as the media would follow our brave soldiers fighting in Iraq to defend our nation and help the people in Iraq.

Part of Jay Jay's assignment included protecting the Green Zone, where many important people stayed. It was one of the relatively safe places, with danger everywhere in Iraq. His active tour of duty in Iraq was over after fifteen months. While there, he met several famous people who were there for the war effort and a chance for freedom for the people of Iraq. It was extremely dangerous, and Jay Jay felt better with his knife, rifle, and a pistol nearby at all times.

He described one of his experiences when an Iraqi woman came to the Green Zone after walking five miles looking for her husband. She feared that her husband was dead and was desperate for information. The soldiers searched her very carefully, as they were fearful that she might have a bomb under her dress. It was not unusual for men to disguise themselves as women and carry bombs to blow up everything and everyone nearby. They had to always be on guard and watch for suicide bombers. Today, surprisingly, even women strap bombs on their bodies and try to blow up everyone for their cause.

Some of the palm trees surrounding the Green Zone needed to be trimmed for better visibility, so the troops could better prevent attacks by the terrorists. Since Jay Jay was a tree man from Daytona Beach, he decided to show the Iraqi soldiers how he could climb up and trim the palm trees. They told him they did it without shoes, and Jay Jay climbed the trees without his shoes. He said he would never try that again.

One day, Jay Jay befriended a young, twelve-year old Iraqi boy and hired him to clean up the trash around the base inside the Green Zone for a dollar a day. The boy would walk along the dangerous streets of Baghdad to the base, in an attempt to earn some money for food for his family. In a short while, his older brother was also helping to clean up the trash around the Green Zone
Shortly thereafter, a newsman from Daytona followed the boy, videotaping his heartwarming story and going to the boy's home to meet with his family. The newsman put together a touching story about the boys' family's life in Iraq, with glimpses into the hard and dangerous times the people were facing daily as the war continued. This story and photos were brought home to America for a view of life in war-torn Iraq. Several times, Jay Jay seemed to be the hometown celebrity, who was interviewed on world and local news.

Sometime later, one of their family members saw Jay Jay on the big screen, talking about Iraq in a film called *9/11*. He didn't even know it, but it was true, and there he was in real life, talking about Iraq. He looked rugged and sounded good, but he did not appreciate this particular screen appearance, as no one had asked for his permission.

Far away back home, the family missed Jay Jay while he was gone during his special missions in the war effort to help the Iraqi people. Many days, Carrie, John, and Logan would visit "Grandma Honey" and swim in her pool. It always made Grandma happy to have them around. Little Logan gave her the name Grandma Honey, and all the grandchildren shared the new name. They spent many hours together as Helen enjoyed talking and sharing her stories with Carrie, who always seemed ready to listen. They said prayers for the safe return of all the troops who were so far from home.

When Logan would come over to visit Grandma Honey, he would pace back and forth around the room on the cell phone, enjoying his conversations with his daddy, who was in a faraway place in Iraq. It was truly a sight that almost made you laugh with joy and cry tears at the very same time. Meanwhile, J. C. (little John) felt lonely and missed his dad as well, and he also needed to hear his dad's voice on the cell phone.

Life went on for the family as Carrie did her wartime duty by keeping up the home front.
Carrie kept the tree business running and always reminded Jay Jay that his family needed him and to keep safe. She kept busy working at the tree business while Jay Jay was away in Iraq, though it was very difficult for everyone back at home. He was one of the many brave soldiers who were able to locate lots of weapons that were ultimately destroyed.

His young sons continued to pray for their dad's safe return. Logan was almost two years old when his dad left to go overseas, and Jay Jay was gone for almost a year and a half. Logan carried around a snapshot of his dad, and when he saw him on TV news, he would put his hand on the TV and cry. When Jay Jay came home from Iraq, Logan would cling to him, letting everyone know, "That's my daddy" and telling Jay Jay, "You can't leave, Daddy."

Anna's husband, John, had always been proud to take all the sisters out to dinner once a week. For a short time, he suffered from colon cancer and received treatments. One evening each week, the family would meet to play a few games of cards. At the same time, they were able to enjoy a social visit at Helen's home. The family was very glad for their time together and appreciated John for making their weekly visits possible. Unfortunately, he had to say good-bye, and sadly, on April 5, 2004, he quietly passed away.

It was tough to be in the hot desert in Iraq, facing the horrific wind and brutal sand storms, with an enemy close at hand. Jay Jay was used to Florida's lush, green land; plentiful lakes; and an ocean fit for surfing. He was used to fishing in the deep waters of the nearby Halifax River, the Atlantic Ocean, and Spruce Creek. Many times, he thought of how nice it would be to be safely home with his family on his little ranch, enjoying peace and quiet, away from the bombing that lit the night skies.

Perilous times were ahead for the Iraqi people and the soldiers, as danger filled the air. One day, a car bomb blew up in the safe area of the Green Zone, killing some innocent Iraqis. Immediately, Jay Jay rushed from the outside shower and quickly called to let everyone at home know that he was safe.

Everywhere Iraq is Full of Danger with each Blast They're Beginning to Wonder how Long it Might Last

While Jay Jay was away, Linda and her students in Orlando sent him many boxes of goodies and personal letters to share with his brave fellow troops. The students showed their support for the brave soldiers and their courageous fight for Iraqi freedom. These young students and underpaid teachers gladly chipped in for personal items and much-needed supplies to help make the soldiers feel comfortable and know they were missed. Jay Jay happily distributed their most welcome care packages and letters to the men in his platoon.

He was able to visit one of Saddam's luxurious places, and some of the troops were able to swim in the inviting pool, cooling off and enjoying some much-needed rest and recuperation. This was, indeed, a terrible time for the Iraqi people, and they needed our country's help to make Iraq a safer place.

During his stay in Iraq, Jay Jay began to learn to speak the language, making many new friends. He was proud to serve his country and believed it would be better to fight the enemy in their own country. This war was very different from any they had every experienced, and the troops hoped to get the situation in Iraq under control as quickly as possible.

Bombs went off daily in the streets, and many innocent bystanders were maimed or killed by the terrorists; each day there were many Iraqi casualties as well as casualties among their own brave soldiers. After a little more than fifteen months of active tour duty, it was time for Jay Jay to return home.

It will always be remembered in history that our troops were there every step of the way. The American soldiers liberated an oppressed people and gave them a chance for a better life. Something we may all want to consider is whether the war in Iraq was warranted or not, and this is a possible question for the future to decide.

With Great Honor, the Troops are Welcomed Home Knowing they Have Left the Danger Zone

Shortly, after he returned from Iraq, Jay Jay visited Linda at the her school in Orlando to thank the teachers and students alike for their prayers and packages. He brought a vehicle to the school and put it in the hall to help him create a somewhat more realistic scene of what the soldiers endured in real life in the war zone. The school set aside one full day so all the classes and teachers could take an hour to talk about some of the events that took place in Iraq. Jay Jay demonstrated how he slept at night while he was on his watch and allowed all the children to take turns in his sleeping bag. In a short few minutes, they had to get up, with little time left for sleep.

It was an emotional day for both Jay Jay and Linda; as they held hands, tears rushed down their cheeks happy smiles spread across their faces. Jay Jay thanked the students and teachers for the thoughtful cards and packages they had sent to the soldiers in his platoon. Jay Jay was very patriotic and continued to serve in the National Guard as an instructor.

On her sixty-second birthday, Helen was in for a big surprise. She came home one evening to find the room in total darkness. She opened the door to her condo and stood there in disbelief when she found some of her close relatives and Len standing there anxiously waiting to shout "Happy Birthday". It was so thoughtful and a happy time for Helen to remember.

New Years Eve at the Biltmore in Coral Gables

It was 2003, and the New Year was soon to arrive. Helen and Len decided to take a holiday trip to Miami for a short visit to see Helen's daughter, Ann, son-in-law, Bruce, and grandchildren. They were excited to welcome in the New Year at the famous and affluent Biltmore Hotel in Coral Gables, Miami. Notably, the hotel was unique in design and situated in nostalgic, beautiful, tropical surroundings. It was unusual to see the little birds swinging in their ornate cages in the hotel lobby. It was nice to know that many famous presidents and dignitaries had stayed at the Biltmore in the past. The hotel's restaurant was a must-stop in the area for its delicious food and beautiful, tropical surroundings. Helen and Len spent some time visiting interesting restaurants and touring Miami.

Orchids were a new hobby for Helen and Len. They took trips to many neighboring towns to buy a variety of tropical orchids to add to their collection. Caring for the flowers was almost a full-time job. They were able to collect a number of different species from all over the world. The orchids had some of the most beautiful blooms, lasting for several weeks and displaying many bright colors.

It's Been a Very Long Time at Spruce Creek; Now It's Time for New Adventures to Seek

After living in the Daytona Beach-Spruce Creek area for more than thirty-five years, three of those years on the ocean, it was time to move along and continue with life's adventures. Helen and Len were looking forward to better things just ahead.

Helen sold her home and had to rent for a while in Pt. Orange, as her new townhouse in Hobe Sound was under construction. In July 2004, Helen made her move to Hobe Sound. It seemed to be more southerly and a little bit warmer on the Treasure Coast of Florida. Len moved in the area to be near Helen as well. However, he soon found the area somewhat quiet, as he wanted more action. He decided to move farther south, to Palm Beach Gardens.

Situated on a small lake, Helen's new home allowed her to spend many evenings watching for the picturesque sunsets and enjoying a quiet peace in her new "Retreat." The development reached out over five hundred acres of peaceful tranquility. It was a good place to hang your hat and get a breath of fresh air, and it felt good to be home. This was a place to relax, and Helen's writing career had begun. Tina's daughter, Linda, moved from New York bought a home on another lake close to the Retreat. Linda's husband, Bobbie, loved the fishing, and they also felt they'd found paradise in Florida.

In summer 2004, they had to face the oncoming hurricane season. Many homes were destroyed, and blue-covered roofs were visible in the area for a period of more than two years. This was mainly a result of the devastating storms causing havoc around Florida. The deadly storms around Hobe Sound seemed to Helen a strange phenomenon, as she'd lived in Florida for more than fifty years.

Could it be that Florida was becoming a home for the catastrophic hurricanes that they had been experiencing?

Helen and Len left the area temporarily, as they feared the storm might strengthen. They traveled to a hotel in Jacksonville, bringing along Cessna, Len's Macaw parrot, so he too would be safe from the hurricane. After they arrived, the hotel's electric power went out, but soon became available in the hotels' main area, when the hotel cranked its generators. Helen had fallen in front of her bank earlier in the week and injured her foot. She found it necessary to get around on crutches and use a wheelchair.

After they settled in, Len was tired and quickly fell asleep. After Helen got into the tub, she was unable to get out because of her injury. A bit desperate to get help, she called for Len, but he was in a deep sleep and did not hear her calls. Cessna, however, heard her and began to squawk very loudly, calling her name over and over. Len finally woke up after hearing all the commotion Cessna was making. Carefully, he assisted Helen out of the bathtub, and Helen petted and thanked Cessna for saving her from spending the night in a very uncomfortable, hard bathtub with her injured leg.

On December 31, 2004, on New Year's Eve, Len sent a limo to pick up Helen in Hobe Sound so she could join him at the Marriott Hotel in Palm Beach Gardens. By mistake, the limo driver took Helen to the wrong hotel and left her waiting there. In the meantime, it was getting late, and Len was patiently waiting. He continued to pace in the hotel lobby, as well as in the street, and he was extremely worried. Meanwhile, Helen was also in the lobby of another hotel waiting. The hour was getting late and she was a bit fearful, being at the wrong place in a strange town waiting for Len. With no sign of Len, she called the limo driver service for some assistance.

This time, Helen arrived safely, and Len was delighted to see her arrive in his waiting arms. Early in the evening, they met their new, interesting friends, Chris and Mike, and were able to share a great evening with wonderful entertainment. It was a time to dance and enjoy a delicious dinner. A young singer who imitated Elton John and was absolutely fabulous was the main entertainment. Chris and Mike continued a very friendly relationship with Helen and Len as time went on.

Many times, Helen and Len enjoyed tasty Greek dinners at Santorini's Restaurant at the Bluffs in Jupiter. They spent a lot of time at the restaurant, eating and visiting with Angelo, the owner. Len loved to talk with Cessna, while Helen said he was her captive audience when she sang to him. When Len found it had become difficult to take care of Cessna, he decided to give the bird to Angelo and his family. It was a little sad to give up his beautiful, talking bird, even though, many times, Cessna behaved like a spoiled child. At first, Angelo kept the cage outside in the front of the restaurant, where Cessna would always attract a great deal of attention, as he would call to everyone passing by.

On one occasion, Angelo provided the restaurant and food for a charitable benefit, and a great deal of people arrived to taste his delicious Greek cuisine. More people had appeared than he had planned, and things got hectic and he found he was short of help. Len and Helen sped into action, helping out by setting the tables, bringing water to the patrons, and clearing the dishes. They were there to help in any way they could. The

Greek music and dancing created a very happy atmosphere, making it a very enjoyable, as well as tiring, evening.

Shopping was always a pleasure when Helen and Len went to Worth Avenue in Palm Beach. It was always interesting to check out the stores and talk about their lovely new designs. Though the prices seemed very high, the shops had the best of everything money could buy. Helen continued to window shop and became very interested in a quaint antique shop.

As she looked in the window, the owner of the shop came out and asked Helen to join him in a glass of champagne while she had a look around. In a very short while, Len, Gary, and Rosemary were looking for Helen, and they too entered the antique shop. They joined in the champagne party and shared interesting conversation while they looked at valuable paintings and antiques.

Sometimes they would meet with Rena and Brandt and Chris and Mike and stop in at Taboo, a famous restaurant in Palm Beach. It always proved to be a fascinating place, as they often saw interesting celebrities visiting from around the world. It was a special evening when Rena and Brandt invited Helen and Len to the Burt Reynolds Museum in Jupiter to enjoy a special event, wherein low-budget directors gave a talk on the movie-making business and making European films. The event proved to be very rewarding, and after the presentation, Helen and Len enjoyed their tour throughout the museum. It was nostalgic and brought back a lot of fond memories of movies from the past.

On another occasion, Len invited a group of people to the River House for drinks and to work on a mini-story for a movie-type production. They discussed the writer's minimal ideas and changed it into an adventure story, with a cast of actors acting out the story in front of a live audience. Helen was chosen to play the role of the mother in the production, while Len directed the group in the movie-type production for a bartender they had just recently met. His story was about a football player he'd met in college. Len and the others assisted the author with new ideas, helping to create and change it into an actual story.

It wasn't long before Len invited another small group to Angelo's Santorini's Restaurant in Jupiter for drinks and dinner and to partake in a screenwriter's review. Again, it was fun for Len and Helen to help an aspiring New York playwright with his story find in different outcomes for his play. The story was about an ethnic Jewish family in an exciting espionage mystery.

It's Such a Happy Day Now that You Have Arrived For We Can Share Your Special Gift of Love Inside

A most joyous occasion for Linda and Peter was the arrival of their beautiful daughter, Emma Leigh, on June 7, 2005. Emma was truly a miracle baby; arriving three weeks early, she was a gift of love, as she could make everyone so happy. The couple had been thinking about how nice it would be to have a little one to love in their life. Deep down, they knew that God must have been listening. Sometime during one of last year's hurricanes, Linda and Peter got close, and she became pregnant. Helen now boasts of having six lovely grandchildren.

A short time later, Len's daughter and family came to North Miami Beach for a family bar mitzvah. They invited Len and Helen to join them at the family affair. It was fun to drive down to South Beach with Len's family to check out the busy nightlife. They decided to enter a nightclub called The Mansions. The club featured multi-rooms, and his family paid a very high price for admittance by buying a bottle of vodka as an entry fee. It was almost impossible to get through the crowded room to find a table to sit down, as the room was dark, the music was very loud, and the tables were crowded close together. Helen began to wonder how these young people could afford to go to such an expensive nightclub.

After a drink or two, they pushed their way through the young crowd, in an attempt to try a few fancy steps, and quickly picked up on the beat of the loud rap music. Three young ladies quickly approached Helen's table after they'd sat back down to praise her dancing. Len's family was quite surprised to see Helen and Len performing so well on the dance floor, especially in a nightclub full of younger men and women. While Helen and Len were dancing, the young people stepped aside to watch them. Before long, some of the young men started dancing alongside Helen back-to-back. While on the dance floor, one young man stopped to shake Len's hand and told him that he was awesome and a fantastic dancer, continuing to dance with him back-to-back. They were not surprised at the attention they were getting because many times they had performed on the dance floor with their fancy steps. Len taught Helen a number of new dance steps, since he had been a choreographer in the movie business at one time.

When Helen returned home, she called her daughter, Ann, in Miami to tell her that she had been out on the town dancing with Len at the Mansions. Ann mentioned that her daughter, Lauren, had also been there at the same time that evening. Sadly, she was in another dark room at the Mansions, and they missed seeing each other. It would have been nice to meet up with Lauren and her friends, but it was not meant to be. It seems like timing is everything in this world.

This was not the first time Helen and Len had made a hit on the dance floor. While living in Daytona Beach, they were invited to an Iranian New Year's Eve party, and a young, professional Iranian singer stopped the music to acknowledge their performance, while doing their style of dancing. The performer asked if they were Iranian but soon realized, after seeing Helen's blonde hair and Len's blonde hair and blue eyes, that they were not of Iranian descent.

While living in Hobe Sound, Helen and Len spent many nights at Bianca's Night Club, where they enjoyed dinner and dancing until the band stopped playing. The music was entertaining, and the dancing provided them a lot of good exercise. Dancing at Bianca's was the highlight of many of their fun-filled evenings.

On New Year's Eve in 2005, Helen and Len joined their friends, Rena and Brandt and Chris and Mike, at the Leopard Lounge in the Chesterfield Hotel in Palm Beach. It was a lovely evening and a night for partying. The maitre de' believed he was taking care of some very famous movie people, and he was. He told the group that he'd held the paparazzi at bay, and they would be waiting outside after midnight for some pictures and an interview. The meal was delicious with outstanding service. During the evening, when Chris went to the ladies' room, the maitre de' asked her when the famous movie star would be arriving. She was so cute as she asked him what was wrong with her. The music was nice, and it seemed like they danced the night away until the clock struck midnight. Helen knew this would b a night to remember. It really was a very special and a joyful night to keep as a nice memory.

In November 2006, Helen prepared to move back to Daytona Beach and be a bit closer to her family, as she was really beginning to miss her children and grandchildren. She got busy collecting extra boxes to start the packing process. After dinner, upon their return to Len's townhouse in Jupiter, they found the gate was locked.

It was about nine in the evening, and there wasn't anyone around. They knew they were in trouble, so Helen bravely told Len she would try to climb over the six-foot fence to open the lock. She piled up the soft boxes and climbed up, putting her foot over the fence, while Len held her up so she wouldn't fall. The pain to her knees was almost unbearable, and she started calling for help. The wooden fence had begun to push into her arthritic knees.

In the darkness of night, a miracle happened, as a man and wife appeared from out of nowhere. The kind man heard Helen's call for help and immediately raced across the street with his wife, baby, and dog close behind.

It was lucky that the man was big and strong, and after sizing up the situation at hand, he lifted Helen up in the air like a rag doll and gently put her down alongside Len. He then proceeded to climb the fence himself and break the lock. Helen hadn't realized her days of climbing fences were over, and she had to learn the hard way that it was time to leave fence climbing for the younger generation.

It's a Good Feeling When We Can Say Ayden's Arrival Makes it a Great Day

Helen now has seven lovely grandchildren, with her newest treasure—the joyous birth of Ayden Justin on June 22, 2006, to Carrie and Jay Jay. Possibly, this may complete the family history that began with two special people, Eva and Frank, in the early 1900s; they will live on in their children and in their children's children. It is such a delight to have loving children and grandchildren to welcome into the world and watch as they enrich their family's lives. After they are all grown and leave home, they will continue to bring happiness and contribute their talents and goodness to the world. Some of the emptiness is gone, as they come home again and again to visit with the grandparents.

The family had come full circle, as Ayden's great-grandmother, Eva, was born on June 20, 1903—2 days and 103 years earlier.

The time has quickly passed, and Helen's children continue to go in different directions, spreading their love as they touch many along life's path. I'm sure their children will do the same as the cycle of life continues.

Ann and Bruce have raised a fine family we can all be proud of. Ann stayed in Miami and has successfully started a small company selling baby quilts with Bible verses. It is a nice feeling to see and hear special words from God and hold them close to your heart.

A SPECIAL MESSAGE TO MY DAUGHTER, ANN

As surely as the sunshine reaches far across the land,
A bright light from above will be glowing in the sand.
Fifty-one happy years have passed since you first came to me;
It's a wonderful feeling watching what you've grown up to be—
Such a kind, devoted, beautiful mother, and a child of God.
I can remember when you were young, playing in the yard,
Celebrating God's magnificent gift in every sweet song
And touching the hearts and minds of many all day long.

From the time when Frankie was a very young lad, he loved to play golf. It was fun and proved to be a challenge. Golf has been his game, and he's collected many trophies, winning tournaments and traveling around the country. After a serious injury to his wrist, he spent many years in the auto industry. He recently returned to playing golf. As he neared his fiftieth birthday, qualifying for the Senior PGA Golf Tour, he was prepared to prove his game once again. Frankie reached his life's dream to play with the best and was, once again, winning many local tournaments. Sadly, it ended too soon, as he died of heart failure in an instant at age fifty. Let us not allow Frankie's passing to be in vain. He knew the Lord as his Savior and was not afraid to admit it. Frankie, aka "the Hammer" had much to teach us. Once he got started on something, he would never quit, and he could sometimes be relentless. He was even able to sell you your own shoes while you were standing in them. He was giving and cared for others along life's way. Always fearless, he was never afraid to chase his dreams, and he was truly successful. He enjoyed the American dream because he found himself and true happiness in playing golf. His family and friends will miss his charm and the laughter that continues to echo in our hearts.

For Frankie, My Son, The Golfer

I do remember you when you were just a young boy,
Filling up my heart with so much happiness and joy.
Always the happy young golfer, playing full of hope,
You talked, laughed, worked and learned how to cope.
At last, when you played and made a hole-in-one,
It was nice to be able to tell you "A job well done."
Our busy life goes on, knowing years have gone by
It's time to stop to tell you, "You're a swell guy."

Today, Linda is a mother and a teacher of elementary school children. She is raising her daughter with her husband, Peter, in Orlando, Florida. Ultimately, she will leave her mark in the lives of her students in the years ahead through her caring and dedication. Her hard work will carry over into her personal life with her family and students alike.

Miss Linda, the Caring Teacher Who Always Puts Her Students First

Your bright smile is as beautiful as the stars can be,
And as each day passes, all the world can easily see:
Linda is so very much like the meaning of her name,
Truly a natural beauty who will surely rise to fame.
She's such a treasure with lots of love she can share
Teaching and touching the hearts of those in her care.

Jay Jay lives in Daytona Beach, Florida, with his wife, Carrie, and their three sons. He continues his tree service business. Jay Jay has a deep love for his country and believes in protecting America at all costs. His reserve unit was activated to serve in Iraq, and since then he has remained in the National Guard, where he continues his duties as an instructor.

Jay Jay, My Courageous Soldier Boy, I Salute You

Somehow when you arrived, I knew from the start
That you would find that special place in my heart.
Such happiness seems to radiate high up in the air,
And it looks like my Jay Jay is tough like a bear.
With the zest for caring, you know the way to live
And so easily the kindness you seem to freely give.
It's very easy to feel proud as each day goes by,
As I'm watching you grow with God up on high.

Meanwhile, Helen has since semiretired from the real estate profession and has moved to Jupiter, Florida. She is having fun in her pursuit of happiness—writing, traveling, and is continuing to enjoy her wonderful family visits. It has been an exciting journey, from a life that began in Poland, some twenty miles from the Ukrainian border, with Frank and Eva.

It is very true that, in our beautiful country, wonderful things can happen, as freedom rings in every heart and home in America. Never give up your hopes and dreams as you set your goals and remember that anything is possible as you, too, can reach for the moon and count your lucky stars.

CPSIA information can be obtained
at www.ICGtesting.com
Printed in the USA
FFHW020348281118
49676102-54048FF